Married
in
12
Months
or Less

Reclaim Your Love Life, Heal Your Heart, and
UNLOCK THE SECRET
to Finding Your Spirit Mate

JACKIE DORMAN

Forefront
BOOKS

Dedication

*T*o my Spirit Mate, David. Your love has changed my life. Thank you for being the string to my kite, the hilt to my blade, and the implementer of all my crazy ideas. We are now, and will always be, an amazing team. I love you.

To my Mama, one of the greatest women I have ever known. Thank you for being my biggest cheerleader. I wish you were here, but I'm so glad you're finally free.

Table of Contents

Introduction

I didn't even have to leave my neighborhood to meet the love of my life. I only had to walk out into my front yard and there he was sweeping his driveway. You are hearing me right. I met and married the boy next door.

Before you get jealous because that sounds so easy and you're thinking how lucky I am, and how you wish that would happen to you, I need to add one tiny little detail. I walked out into my front yard and *yelled* at the man who is now my husband.

Yep—I tore his head clean off.

You probably have some questions, so let me tell you the whole story.

During my divorce from my first husband, I lived on a quiet cul-de-sac full of overpriced townhouses. I had no idea that anyone was moving in next door. Quite honestly, I was worried that I could no longer afford to live there just on my income and was seriously considering moving out. My everyday life was filled with all the fear of the unknown that every divorcing woman feels, especially those with children.

My daughter, six years old at the time, was playing outside with a neighbor. It was a beautiful Saturday afternoon, and I was busy doing my "mom" stuff. After a short amount of time, my daughter's friend came to complain that she had no one to play with anymore.

I asked her why she wasn't playing with my daughter, to which she replied, "She only wants to play with the new girl!"

The new girl? I thought. *Who's the new girl?*

I went outside to see what was going on, and my baby was nowhere to be seen. I ran around to the back, but there was still no sight of her. I started to freak out. She had never left the yard before on her own, and I'd just received an email alert that we had a registered sex offender living in the neighborhood, so naturally my mind went right to the worst-case scenario.

Finally, as I'm running around the cul-de-sac like my hair's on fire, screaming her name, here she came with a cute little blonde who was obviously "the new girl."

"Where have you been?" I demanded.

"At her house," my daughter replied.

"Oh, really? Well, you know you aren't supposed to leave the yard." Still upset from my frantic search, I feigned politeness to this small new neighbor.

"When did you move in?" I asked.

"Today," she said. I asked her what her mom and dad's names were. "Oh, I only live with my dad," she replied. "My parents are divorced."

At this moment, here appeared the "dad" talking to another neighbor in his driveway. Still full of crazy, bitter-lady-next-door adrenaline, I stormed over to him, interrupted the conversation, and very non-politely introduced myself: "I'm Jackie and this is *my* daughter and if she's at *your* house she's there without *my* permission!"

With that announcement, I turned on my heels and strutted away. I was pretty proud of myself. *I told him,* I thought. *How dare he let my six-year-old come over to his house? He's a complete stranger. Didn't he think to ask her if her mother knew where she was? A WOMAN would have known to do that.*

I felt smug. I'd put him in his place and shown him the correct protocol for playing with the neighbors. Later on, as I was leaving to run errands, another neighbor stopped me; you know the type, every neighborhood has one—the gossip.

She managed to know everything that was going on. Sometimes I wondered if she went through our garbage while we slept. I'm pretty sure she knew about my divorce before I did. "Hey, you were pretty hard on that new guy, don't you think?" she said.

"Huh? Who, me?" I replied.

"Yeah," she continued, "he's really nice. He's a single dad of two, and he's a schoolteacher." She said it really slowly as if, *How could you talk to a schoolteacher like that? They're our American heroes!* "And," she said, pausing for emphasis, "he's a Christian." She smiled with glee. She knew with that statement she'd hit the mother lode.

I frowned. My conscience started twitching.

She didn't miss a beat. "He teaches at a *Christian* school and works at that big *church* in town . . . " Then she went in for the kill. "Aren't you a *Christian* too?" She asked this while looking at me with big, innocent eyes.

So now I felt like a total jerk, which was obviously every bit her intention.

I didn't even have the patience to answer so I just nodded and hurried off to my car. I began to rally myself. *I wasn't that mean, was I? Surely a protective mother isn't a bad thing, right? What does she know, anyway? He could be a serial killer,* I assured myself. *He did look nice (and cute,* my inner teenager reminded me). *Yikes! What have I done?*

You know what they say: "When you assume, you make an *ass* out of you and out of me." Well, I definitely did that but thank goodness my big head got another chance.

A week later, I got the opportunity to apologize, and David, the new neighbor, accepted. We began a friendship that four months later turned into a romance and then into a marriage. In eight months, I went from yelling at him in the front yard to saying "I do" at the altar.

Now, fourteen years later, we realize just how perfectly matched we really are, and by perfectly, I mean nobody else could ever put up with either one of us. It was as if we were created for each other, because in a very real way, we were.

I don't believe this kind of passion and compatibility is something that only happens every once in a while, and only to some super lucky people. It also doesn't happen accidentally. It happens by design and with intention.

I believe you've been highlighted by heaven for a divine appointment, a date with destiny, one that will alter the trajectory of your life not just now, but for generations to come. Someday as we are looking back over our lives, there will be certain experiences, opportunities, and decisions that we will be able to point to as the times when something significant happened that changed us forever. I believe if you choose it, this has the power and potential to be one of those times in your life and in the lives of all the women who come after you.

Against All Odds

There are millions of books—somewhere upward of 690 million—sold every year, but you just so happened to find this book. Since those odds are clearly not in your favor as a reader or mine as an author, something beyond "the math" must be at work.

I know you may think it was a coincidence you picked up this book. After all, you just happened to notice it on your daily Target run (I know you, girl) or perhaps it was innocently sitting on the counter at a relative's house or poking its controversial little head out of your friend's purse at lunch. More than likely, the bold title is what caused you to do a double take. You might have laughed out loud, or even rolled your eyes a little, but you still just "had to see" what the heck this book was all about, even if it were just to refute its contents at your next girls' night out over a half-bottle of wine. For the sake of argument, let's just call it curiosity.

But the truth is, because of the odds against you, you didn't find this book at all—you were drawn to it. For lack of a better way to say it, it found you.

Heaven Is Listening

This might sound a little hooky-spooky, but women tell me over and over again that at the moment their lives intersected with mine, they had just been praying about their love lives. Now, let's be honest; when some of them say that they had just been praying, what they really mean is they had just been yelling, cussing, crying, and shaking their fist at the heavens, Bruce Almighty style. They were having a momentary meltdown where they could no longer pretend that they weren't sick and tired of feeling lonely, left out, unwanted, unchosen, and just plain angry, sad, and frustrated with their singleness.

They were "wondering" out loud to God and anyone else who would listen—"What's wrong with me?" "Why can't I find someone to love me?" "When is it going to be my turn?" "Where are all the good guys?" They say it's right at that moment that I show up, sometimes before the tears are even dry, out of the clear blue sky like some mystical matchmaking Nanny McPhee.

Often I show up in their text messages from a friend asking them, "Have you ever heard of Jackie Dorman?" I also show up on their social media feed in the form of a shared video or post, and nowadays I even show up on radio—which they tell me they normally *never* listen to anymore.

> I know it's hard to believe after everything you've been through, but God is emotionally involved in your life. Heaven is listening.

Regardless of how my voice reaches them in that moment, more than a few of them believe it's a direct answer from heaven to the cries of their heart. I completely agree. I know it's hard to believe after everything you've been through, but God is emotionally involved in your life. Heaven is listening. So it isn't just a coincidence.

I can't believe in coincidences because I have had too many personal experiences to prove that they don't exist. I no longer believe our lives are big, random, serendipitous free-for-alls. Instead I believe our lives are constantly unfolding, exquisitely written masterpieces, chock-full of adventure and excitement with invitation after invitation to more.

At every page turn, there's a new opportunity to receive all that God has stored away just for us. This is one of those opportunities. It reminds me of that little pop-up message on your cell phone that tells you, usually at the most inconvenient and random times, that there is a new operating system available. I don't know about you, but that usually happens to me when I am nowhere near Wi-Fi and don't have the time to take advantage of the download that's available.

But it waits for me. It reminds me, every once in a while, that it's still there and still available. Eventually I am perfectly positioned at home with Wi-Fi phone fully charged, ready to receive the upgrade.

This Is Your Invitation

In my own life, every single time something life-changing was about to happen to me, it started with a book. Sometimes I got that book long before I was ready to receive the message that it carried.

For instance, my mother recently passed away. It was a very traumatic loss for me. I didn't know how to navigate it or who to talk to about how I was feeling, and I began to cry out to God. One day as I was having my daily cryfest, I noticed a book sitting on my bookshelf.

I have a lot of books from all different seasons of my life. Some I have read, and some I have not. This particular book was simply titled *Heaven*, and I remembered instantly that I'd gotten it as a free bonus book from a book club that I was in more than twenty years ago. As a bonus book, that means that I didn't even pick it; apparently, it picked me.

I have purged my book collection many times over the years; donated books; loaned books to friends who, of course, never returned them; and somehow this book has made the cut every time. I have moved eleven times since I received that book in the mail in 1997, and yet it stayed with me until I was finally ready to receive its message.

> When the student is ready, the teacher will come.

With all my heart I believe the saying that when the student is ready, the teacher will come. You are ready. Your heart has been primed to receive the message on these pages because God has been preparing your heart for years for this very moment. You are being invited into a relationship upgrade.

It's Time for a Plot Twist

I have learned during twenty-four years of teaching women that the subject of this book isn't simply an unhealed place. For many women it's an open, infected, and festering heart wound filled with all kinds of "dis": disillusionment, disappointment, and discouragement.

I already surmised that calling this movement "Married in 12 Months or Less" was going to get some people up in their feelings, and by that I mean it was going to really tick them off.

I even argued with God about it. "We are going to hit a nerve with this branding," I told him.

"It's not branding, Jackie; it's my promise," he told me.

"A promise? You mean this title is a literal declaration?" I started to get really nervous now. "One year or less? Engaged? Married? You mean to a good guy, right, God?"

"Yes, I mean to a great guy!" he confirmed. "A match made in heaven! When you have a healthy, healed, and whole heart, it doesn't have to take a long time."

I immediately began to think of all the marriages I had seen over the years that had happened quickly—and I've seen more than a few. As a result, I have become a firm believer that there are two types of marriages that happen fast: the toxic, codependent, crazy ones, and the undeniably supernatural ones. I've had both kinds. The tragic kind and the God kind. God doesn't write sad love stories, but until we learn how to fully surrender the pen, we definitely do.

The Ancient of Days Has Ancient Ways

I believe we're living in a time when God is restoring not just our own foundations, but the foundations of generations. I believe that every one of you reading this book has the opportunity to be a kinsman redeemer and that whatever negative patterns have been running in your family in the area of love and relationships can run out with you.

So many people have so much confusion and chaos around the area of relationships, especially romantic relationships. People are finding it hard to connect, and it's a global problem. It's ironic since we have never been more connected because of the rise of technology and social media, and yet we still can't seem to find one another. And when we do, we can't seem to really connect with others on a deeper level.

Even in China, a country where men outnumber women, some companies are giving single women "dating leave" in hopes they'll be able to find their partner. (So clearly, "no single men" isn't the problem.) People everywhere are having trouble in this area, not just in your country, city, or community.

> "When you have a healthy, healed, and whole heart, it doesn't have to take a long time."

Nowadays we let technology and apps do the dirty work of sorting out suitors. But it's time for us to take a different course. The ways we have been doing things for so long aren't working. The modern ways have let us down time and time again. I know it can get us thinking there is something wrong with us, but what if there is just something wrong with the culture around us? If we're not able to form attachments with the opposite sex, at least not for the long-term, then certainly there has to be a healthier way.

Falling in love is not meant to be this hard! I know so many people long for a simpler time. Something has got to give, and it's got to give soon. Deep in our hearts we know there is more because there is something hardwired in us that tells us this is not how it's supposed to be. There's a better way.

Go stand at the crossroads and look around.
Ask for directions to the old road,
The tried-and-true road. Then take it.
Discover the right route for your souls.
—Jeremiah 6:16 MSG

I think we can all agree that we're at a crossroads as a society. This passage from Jeremiah is telling us that the ancient of days has ancient ways. When we're confused, lost, sick, and tired of being sick and tired, we can ask for directions to the good way, the better way, the ancient way. I believe that good road will lead us back to our relationship roots—back to the real purpose of marriage, back to the highest versions of ourselves, and back to the authentic masculine and feminine.

God is making matches and restoring family right now. I believe that 100 percent. Every week, I receive news of clients going on dates after decades of nothing, having good interactions with the opposite sex, and getting engaged and married to the love of their life.

God wants to heal the relationships in your life, starting with your relationship with him, then with yourself, and then with others—in that order. These beautiful God-written love stories are not just between you and the man of your dreams, contrary to popular belief. They originate between you and God, and your relationship with your future husband is just a beautiful extension and continuation of that love story.

> God wants to heal the relationships in your life, starting with your relationship with him, then with yourself, and then with others—in that order.

I know beyond a shadow of a doubt that these love stories are available to everyone who wants one but not without some heart-work. God doesn't love me more than he loves you. God is playing matchmaker more than ever, and he wants to make a match for *you*. This book will show you how to let him. It's time to stop going it on your own. It's his desire to reconstruct marriage and family and he wants that reconstruction to start with you. But you have to give him permission to do that for you.

If you're ready to allow him to supernaturally work in your life, pray this prayer:

Father God,

I give you permission to search me and to reveal anything in my heart that does not belong to my true feminine identity. Anything that is hindering me from living the big, beautiful life you created me to live. Holy Spirit, I invite you into the darkest areas of my heart. Show me the areas that are still wounded and still hurting. The areas that are holding me back from fully giving and receiving love. When you reveal these broken places to me, I covenant with you to release them into your care and to respond with forgiveness and repentance. I set aside this season of my life for a time of healing and wholeness and ask the Holy Spirit to take charge of this process. I ask that you dwell with me and in me. I need you. I cannot heal myself. I want to be free from the past, free to be who I truly am. Help me to become the amazing woman you have created me to be.

Show me the lies I have believed about myself, men, marriage—even the lies I have believed about you. Teach me the Greater Truth, teach me your ways, teach me how to love, and teach me how to live abundantly.

Teach Me, Show Me, Heal Me, and Grow Me,

Amen

Chapter One

What Is It that You Really Want?

I can't count the number of women I've talked to over the years with crazy horror stories of past relationships. I've heard unbelievable stories of rejection, heartbreak, and stories of infidelity and scandal that would rival the plot of a Lifetime movie. Most of these women throw in the towel and say, "Never again! I'm done forever! I'm getting a cat!" But just like the infamous cast of *Sex and the City*, they're never really done. They always—and I mean, *always*—try again.

No matter how much disappointment, how many times you've thought "he's the one" (only to have him ask out your friend), how many penis pics have been sent to your dating app inbox, how many awful first dates you've been on, how many times you've met Prince Alarming instead of Prince Charming . . . you still keep coming back for more.

> You have every letter of the alphabet *after* your name, but you still want M-R-S *before* your name.

Are you kidding me? Are you nuts? Didn't you get the memo? This is the 21st century. We're liberated women. We're empowered. Women don't need no man!

I mean, seriously, it's not that you're desperate. You're beautiful. You're intelligent. You're successful. You have "award-winning" in your bio on your company's website. You're educated. You have every letter of the alphabet *after* your name, but you still want M-R-S *before* your name.

You still want a man. You still want to be married, even though you might have an amazing career. You still want to be a mother, no matter how many times your one year of "women's studies" in college says you don't need to be a wife and mom to be fulfilled. You still want it.

You might hate yourself for it. Women tell me all the time that they feel ashamed for still wanting this. You might be sneaking this book past family members or roommates or strangers on an airplane.

It's sad, but so many women tell me they can't talk to anyone about this desire anymore, especially divorced women or women under/over a certain age, without people telling them they should just enjoy their unmarried lives. That's easy for others to say considering most of those advice givers are married. (Probably unhappily married, which is why they envy you not having to deal with their annoying spouse.)

Women have been shamed for too long for wanting to be married. They have been shamed by modern culture for not being empowered enough to have outgrown that "archaic" desire and shamed by family and friends for not being independent enough to be happily single. They've even been shamed by spiritual communities for not loving God enough to be content in what seems like the never-ending waiting room.

So why do *you* want a husband? You want one, or else you wouldn't have picked up this book.

I once had a matchmaking client who had been married five times (yes, five). After hearing about the disasters her love life had been, I point-blank asked her why she wanted to be married again after everything she had been through.

She looked at me and said, "I don't know. I just still believe God has a good marriage for me."

Maybe you're like my client. No matter how many times you get your heart broken, even if your relationship resume looks like a really bad CARFAX report with wreck after wreck listed, you keep trying. Or maybe you're the opposite. Maybe you're the one who never got picked. Perhaps you've had crush after crush end up with someone else. You've had a string of first dates that never turned into second dates, or you've never even been asked on an actual date at all.

Either way, you've been met with failure after failure. So why are you downloading that dating app yet again? Why are you going to *another* singles event? Why are you binge-watching Hallmark movies, dreaming about the day it's finally going to be your turn?

You Were Created for This

The reason is simple: You were created for this. As the feminine of God, you naturally desire to reconnect with your masculine counterpart.

If you're a woman, you were born to embody the feminine of God. I want to tell you something about your femininity, about your gender—gender was instituted as part of God's original and perfect plan.

God said, "Let us make mankind in our image, male and female let us make them." So the divine community—Father, Son, and Holy Spirit—is both masculine and feminine.

Remember, God is not a man, even though he's depicted as a man (which is part of the reason we don't see ourselves through the lens of divinity as women). But he is not a man, he is not a person, he is not even human. God is a spirit. The attributes of both genders are contained within the spiritual community of heaven.

As a woman, you were created to represent the feminine attributes of God. That's part of my purpose of writing this book—helping you step back into that authentic feminine. Because when you step back into that, your influence and impact on the world will be unlimited. A lot of us women have disconnected from our femininity. We equate being a woman with weakness. We sometimes believe it's even dangerous to be a woman. Many of us have been exploited or used because we were born female.

I want to help you make peace with the way God made you and help you step back into God's original plan for your life. That's what Jesus came to do. He came to reconcile us as sons and daughters.

That's what the cross does. It reconciles us first back to God, but it also has the power to reconcile us back to ourselves and then to one another. When I know who I am to myself, I know who to be to others in partnership, relationship, and community. That was God's original plan—relationship and community.

Simply put, God wanted a family. That's why he created us in the first place. You've been created for love, both to love and be loved. In the same way God exists in community—Father, Son, and Holy Spirit—he wants us to exist in community too.

In the Beginning

So let's talk about the seven days of creation. You know that story, right? God's speaking. He's using his words to create. "Let there be light. Let there be land. Let there be water. Let them separate. Let there be mountains and oceans and trees and birds and life in the sea and beasts on the land." He's speaking all these amazing things into being, and it's all happening with just a few words from his mouth.

> He formed us. He's emotionally involved with us. And the same level of care he took with that first person, he took with you.

When we get to the sixth day, he says "Let us make man." I really love what God does on this day. All the things we think are so amazing and majestic are things he spoke into existence. I don't know about you, but I have cried while standing before the beauty of God's creation. There are not even words in the English language to describe the beauty of oceans, mountains, and forests. We just keep saying, "Wow. That's amazing. That's awesome. Wow." When it came to making us, the ancient text says God didn't simply speak; instead, he crafted us with his own hands.

I want you to see how intentional God is with his family. He didn't just speak us into existence—he formed us. He's emotionally involved with us. And the same level of care he took with that first person, he took with you.

He knit you together in your mother's womb, just like he formed Adam out of the dust and breathed life into him. He was just as invested with all the beautiful sparkling threads he used to make the amazing masterpiece that is you.

So here we have Adam. He's been formed on the sixth day and God brings all these animal friends around to hang out with him. Adam is having fun naming all these animals in a beautiful utopia in perfect relationship with God. Sounds incredible.

But God looks at this and says, "This ain't good."

I should mention that after God created all those other amazing things with the words of his mouth every day up until this point, God was like, "This is good!" The word "good" here means "I like this! This is done. This is complete. No tweaking necessary!"

> God himself is saying right here that he wasn't enough for man, that man needed compan- ionship with someone who was like him.

But on *this* day, he takes a look at Adam hanging out with the animals in this sweet garden that he planted just for him and says, "This isn't finished. Something is missing."

The Father turns to the other members of the heavenly family and says, "It's not good for man to be alone."

Alone? Did I miss something? Did I fall asleep again while reading the Bible? I do that sometimes. Adam's not alone. He's surrounded by creation. He was in the presence of God like none of us have ever experienced. It's like that song "In the Garden"; God walked with him, and talked with him, and called him his own. We've never experienced God that way. We've only had a teeny-tiny taste of what that's like, but that was Adam's everyday reality.

So what God was really saying was, "It's not good for man to have a life that doesn't include an interdependency with his own kind." Relationship with Father, Son, and Holy Spirit wasn't enough. Just as the divine family is in relationship with their own kind, Adam needed a relationship with his own kind.

That rather large, often-overlooked detail should debunk all the voices that tell you that God should be enough for you, shaming you because you want something with human skin on it, saying there's something wrong with you if God doesn't satisfy all your relational needs. God himself is saying right here that he wasn't enough for man, that man needed companionship with someone who was like him.

Woman—God's Gift to Man

God says, "Man needs a suitable partner. He needs a helper. He needs to exist in partnership just like we do. We're one in three parts. Let's make him the same as us."

Enter the first surgery. God puts Adam to sleep and removes his rib. The choice of body part here is very significant.

God could have picked any part of Adam he wanted. He could have removed a toe, an appendix (we don't need that anyway), or even a testicle (there are plenty of men who survive with half a set). But, no; God chose a rib.

The rib implies the chest, or the heart. God removed the feminine from the side of the masculine to indicate that she is to be an equal partner, to walk beside him and work not for him but with him. As you can see, the feminine was already inside Adam. God removed the feminine from the masculine so it could dwell in its own vessel in partnership and companionship.

If it helps you to understand this, think of John 3:16 (KJV)—"God so loved the world that he gave his only begotten son." Hold up: I thought we were all sons and daughters? What does he mean his "*only* son"? The important word in that verse is "begotten," which means to "birth from" or "remove from" himself. Yes, we are his sons and daughters, but we were created from creation. God removed Jesus from himself.

Just as Jesus was removed from the Father, we as women were originally taken out of man. Now in the whole cycle of life, all life comes out of women. In 1 Corinthians 11:11–12, we see a complete creation cycle—woman came out of man and man now comes from woman; without each other, we're not complete.

So God fashions Eve and brings her to Adam, and as soon as Adam wakes up, God doesn't even have to introduce her.

"At last!" the man exclaimed. "This one is bone from my bone, and flesh from my flesh!"

—GENESIS 2:23 NLT

Adam immediately recognizes Eve as a part of himself that has been taken out and is standing right here in front of him. He calls her "woman."

I've always thought of the word "woman" as "the womb of God and mankind"—the creator, the birther. That's what the feminine does. We are the creators. We are the intuitives. We represent the heart of God in so many ways.

For example, when a man gives a woman his seed, she gives him a baby. Back in the olden days, when men hunted and women gathered, they would give us the kill and we would give them a meal—sustenance, nourishment. If they give us a house, we make it a home where people can be nurtured and grow into their full potential. We receive what man gives us, we transform it, and we give it back to him better than it was originally.

> That's what the feminine does. We are the creators. We are the intuitives.

This is not just what we do; this is who we are, but we've disconnected from this identity. We are able to take what is given to us and make it into something so much more. My background as a media and business consultant has shown me firsthand the power of the feminine to create change. I saw time and time again investors refusing to give micro-loans to men in Third World countries and emerging nations. They only gave them to women. And the reason is because they know from experience that the feminine, the women, will take a loan and they will create something with it. They don't just consume it for themselves. They will take it and they will make it into something that can feed the whole community and benefit the whole country. Something that will better everyone.

That's what the feminine does. We're great collaborators. We create bigger things. We're visionaries in such a strong sense of the word, but many of us have not been taught to value being a woman and the amazing gift of femininity. Instead, we've been taught just to endure being born a girl and happily accept a lesser position in the world. But that's not what God had in mind. He knew we were an important addition to the family with a very vital role to play.

Chapter Two

I Am Woman,
Hear Me Roar

*R*emember that God said man couldn't do what he was created to do alone? That he needed a helper? The word "helper" is the Hebrew word "ezer." It's used twenty-one times in the Bible, including nineteen times for the divine intervention of God. The other two times in the Bible, the word "ezer" is used for—wait for it—"woman."

If you've spent much time around religious circles, you've probably heard women described quite differently than that. Depending on where you come from, you might have heard a woman described as a glorified cook/domestic servant/chauffeur/baby factory. Sometimes we get the weird title of "helpmeet."

> God knew the masculine needed the counterbalance of the feminine and that's why he created women.

While that's not *technically* incorrect, we tend to downplay the full power of the word "ezer." The context in the original language doesn't mean "helper" as in servant, but as in a much-needed and equal complementary counterpart.

Whenever "ezer" is used to describe God, it means God as deliverer, when he is showing up as savior and rescuer in a dire time of need. Ezer is a warrior. It can also be translated as "rescue, to save" and "to be strong."

As we all know from personal experience, most guys are capable of doing dumb things (especially when there are friends and beer involved). A study published in the *BMJ (British Medical Journal)* titled "The Darwin Awards:

Sex Differences in Idiotic Behaviour" found "men are more likely to engage in risky behavior, often at the risk to their own health and finances"[1] (as if we don't all know that). This study was largely based on The Darwin Awards, sarcastically named after Charles Darwin, who popularized the idea of evolution via natural selection. The awards salute the improvement of the human gene pool by honoring those who accidentally remove themselves from it through acts of dangerous stupidity, for lack of a better term. The "awards" go overwhelmingly to men. God knew the masculine needed the counterbalance of the feminine and that's why he created women.

If you have been around men and boys for any length of time, you know that without the influence of women in their lives, they get themselves into a lot of trouble. They pee on electric fences to see what will happen, they wrestle crocodiles, they choke one another to see who passes out first, and they take hot pizza trays out of the oven with their bare hands because oven mitts are for "sissies."

There is a hashtag on social media of #mendoingstupidthings. If you search it, you can dive down the rabbit hole of videos, photos, and stories of men doing everything from chugging beer through their nose to car surfing atop moving vehicles. When I see grown men acting like frat boys, convinced they're indestructible, I know they probably don't have a lot of good female influence in their lives.

I don't want you to get the wrong idea: Woman wasn't created to control man or save man. For many of you, this mentality is the problem in the first place. God created woman to be a strong *partner* for man. Think of it as your left hand and your right hand. One is usually physically stronger than the other, but the opposite hand might be more dexterous and possess greater fine motor skills. In any case, it takes both to effectively complete most tasks because where one is weak, the other is strong and vice versa. Simply put, man and woman are better together.

> You can almost imagine Adam saying, "Hey, girl. Don't worry. I'm coming for you if we're ever torn apart. No matter what it takes, I'm going to find you again."

In addition to being man's strong and capable counterpart, we learn in Proverbs 31:27 in the New International Version that the valiant woman "watches over the ways of her household." Unfortunately, this is another passage that is usually translated in a way that's not doing the original language justice. The word for "watches over" is "tsaphah," which is also used as a military term for the guard of a city or a military encampment. It's used for God watching over people, nations, and situations. The word conveys the idea of a watchman who looks far beyond the horizon and warns of coming danger.

Even the phrase "ways of her household" is undersold here. The word means "watching someone travel." The woman in this passage isn't just running her kids' soccer carpool and packing Pinterest-perfect lunches; she's monitoring the spiritual atmosphere and strategizing on how to lead her family and her lineage through the traps and snares of the wicked one, into their divine destiny.

She's the prayer warrior of her household, fighting spiritual battles in intercession and guarding the future of those around her and all those that will come after her.

You're probably thinking by now that women are pretty badass, right? Well, yes, but I just want to be clear that we are equals with men, not their superiors.

There is no hierarchy implied by God calling us "ezer." God's not saying women were put on this earth to be executive assistants to men, but we also aren't meant to be their managers. That doesn't mean a woman should never help or support her husband, but it does mean that, contrary to what we've been taught for thousands of years, women were not created subservient to men.

As women, we are equal partners who, together with man, are able to fulfill the grand plan of God for his family on Earth. Neither of us can do it alone, but together we are unstoppable.

Dun, Dun, *DUUUNNNN*

In the very next verse of Genesis(2:24), the narrator, Moses, picks right up after Adam's "bone of my bone and flesh of my flesh" speech and says, "For this reason will a man leave his mother and father and be united unto his wife and the two shall *again* be as one."

For *what* reason will a man leave his mom and dad and go find his ezer? For the reason that man is incomplete without his warrior bride and needs her in order to fulfill his God-given purpose on Earth.

I don't know about you, but when I read that last verse, it's almost like it's foreshadowing that there's trouble coming. It's like hearing the Darth Vader theme out of nowhere and knowing that something is about to go terribly wrong. Now that the masculine and feminine have been separated out of one body and come back together as one in marriage, something is going to happen to separate them again.

You can almost imagine Adam saying, "Hey, girl. Don't worry. I'm coming for you if we're ever torn apart. No matter what it takes, I'm going to find you again."

That's really where we are today because that's exactly what happened. I could tell you the whole story or you could go read it for yourself. Here's the annotated version—there's a tree, there's a cold-hearted snake, there's some forbidden fruit (that was apparently to *die* for), and there's a really bad decision that alters this beautiful God-written love story.

The Saddest Story Ever Told

Adam and Eve made the choice not to trust God and deviate from his perfect plan. And it didn't just disconnect them from God; it disconnected them from each other. It separated them on spiritual, emotional, and relational levels.

Not only them, but everyone since them has been subject to the consequences of their choice and has experienced the same separation.

As a result of Adam and Eve's fatal decision, God knew the way they saw things was now forever changed, including the way they saw each other. He warned them, saying, "Because you chose this path, Man, you're going to dominate and rule over Woman, no longer seeing her as my gift to you and your co-equal. Instead of protecting and providing for her, you're going to want to conquer her, possess her, and use her for your own selfish desires. Woman, instead of nurturing, helping, and influencing, you're going to want to manipulate and control. You're going to exert your power through deception and seduction to get Man and keep Man right where you want him."

The Beginning of "Dis"

The curse that resulted from Adam and Eve's decision introduced all kinds of "dis" into the world and into our relationships—disconnection, disillusionment, disobedience, discouragement, distrust, disappointment, dishonor, dysfunction, and so forth.

No matter how much men and women hurt one another in these inherited shame-based identities originating from sin, we continue to gravitate toward one another because we were created for one another. But under the effects of these counterfeit identities, we have a twisted love/hate thing going on.

We can't live with one another, and we can't live without one another. It's like sleeping with the enemy. Everyone on either side is sleeping with one eye open, just waiting for the other person to deceive us, hurt us, and/or betray us.

This is where so many people are in their relationships, their dating lives, and even their marriages right now. It reminds me of what I call the Pit Bull Principle.

Pit bulls are amazing dogs. They're sweet, kind, and intelligent. They make great pets and companions, but because people with nefarious purposes have taught some of them to be aggressive, they have gotten a really bad reputation with most people. Many apartments won't even let you have a pit bull or a pit bull mix on the premises.

Because of this, many people who would like to give a pit bull a chance are always wondering in the back of their minds if they will end up with a bad one.

Men and women are going around with their heads full of dating, relationship, and marriage horror stories, believing that the other is potentially very dangerous but rolling the dice anyway and hoping they will get lucky and be one of the few who get a "good" one. I have so many matchmaking clients whose love lives are being held hostage by the fear that there are very few (if any) good men out there and finding one is like looking for a needle in a haystack. This scarcity mindset can cause a lot of trouble because it creates a guilty-until-proven-innocent dynamic that is very hard to overcome. This is why so many people cannot let their guard down and let love in.

Chapter Three

Now We Got
Bad Blood

*W*e shouldn't be surprised. The effects of these prejudiced belief systems are showing up exactly as God warned us. The "state of the union" between men and women has been deteriorating for thousands of years. The innate appreciation that the masculine and feminine once had for one another has been lost. The seamless partnership we enjoyed in the garden is all but gone.

For everyone who hates how women were treated in the Bible, this is why. You need to know that wasn't God's plan for his daughters.

Man began to dominate, and instead of respecting and honoring God's gift of woman, he began to use and abuse her for his own pleasure and purposes. Woman retaliated with her own more subtle form of domination, and the infamous "battle of the sexes" was on. What started as a beautiful partnership between complementary opposites soon fell into dysfunction and chaos.

So if men and women have become mortal enemies, how are they still getting married? How have they been getting married since we left the garden?

The post-sin pattern didn't just affect how men and women saw one another—it changed the entire paradigm of marriage. Men and women were cast into opposition, and the corrupted masculine began to dominate the corrupted feminine.

Marriage became a business transaction and women were the product. Sounds really romantic, doesn't it. The idea of requiring a woman's consent for a marriage wasn't even introduced until a 12th-century monk got the crazy idea that marriage should be consensual. Most of the time, women were expected to marry whomever their father or guardian chose for them.

If a man was of a high social standing, a woman was valued on her ability to provide him heirs, increased status, additional wealth, titles, and land. If a man was of a lower class, he wanted her ability to do hard labor and provide as many extra hands as possible to help around the farm, the fishing boats, or whatever profession the family was involved in.

In all cases, barrenness (the inability to have children) was grounds for a man to divorce his wife or take a second wife in much of the world until relatively recently. Many people will remember Henry VIII, the English king who created a new religion in order to divorce, annul, and behead his way through six wives in his quest for a male heir.

The post-sin pattern didn't just affect how men and women saw one another—it changed the entire paradigm of marriage.

Women who were able to bear children could, on average, expect to have between six to seven—assuming they survived any possible complications in pregnancy and childbirth and lived long enough to reach that number.

After *centuries* of this, women didn't have many choices. With very few professions available to women, they needed to marry in order to keep a roof over their heads and not bring dishonor or become a burden to their family.

This is where Jane Austen and authors like her in the 1800s got fodder for all their books—getting married was to a woman what getting a job was to a man. In Jane Austen's last novel, *Persuasion*, the heroine Anne Elliot is twenty-seven and coming down to the wire on her clock to find a husband. The other characters in the book clearly pity her, and Anne's perceived aging-out is a main theme of the book.

You might think that's just for 1800s literature, but these ideas have been passed down through generations—ideas that say, "It's too late," "You're timestamped," and "Better beat your expiration date!"

I had a client, Kasey, who was also twenty-seven, just like Anne Eliot. Also like Anne Eliot, Kasey was unmarried although everyone in the small town around her had gotten married at eighteen, straight out of high school, and already had a few kids. This left Kasey feeling damaged and rejected, as if she were too far behind and couldn't catch up.

I asked Kasey what she had been doing since high school. She told me that she had traveled the world doing humanitarian missionary work. She was now about to graduate with a master's degree in nursing, making her a nurse practitioner, almost the equivalent of a physician. I asked her another question—if she thought her high school girlfriends who had gotten married at eighteen and were now mothers had traveled the world or gotten higher education degrees.

She said, "No, they haven't."

So I asked her if she thought that was a fair comparison.

It was only then that she realized that while she had not achieved a marriage or a family yet, she had other accomplishments, and she still had plenty of opportunities to become a wife and mother.

Kasey's story shows how much shame is still tied to this fear of becoming an "old maid." We feel like we need to have that ring (and babies, for that matter) by a certain age or we've missed our chance forever.

As you can imagine, in this corrupted system, abuse and oppression were rampant. Women had little recourse if they were in an unsafe marriage, let alone a loveless marriage. Divorce was almost unheard of and scandalous when it did happen, usually thrusting the woman and her family into social disgrace. Anything that a woman brought into the marriage (including money and other assets) and any children resulting from the marriage were considered the man's property by default.

These things and others were the catalyst for women's suffrage in the late 1800s and early 1900s, also called First Wave Feminism. This led to the continuation of women seeking to gain the right to own property, have access to good jobs, have the right to marry for love (or not marry at all), and seek "reproductive freedom" in Second and Third Wave Feminism.

Even if you don't agree with the tactics or ideologies behind these women's movements, I think we can all see from the course of history how they came to be.

That painful pattern has continued, sometimes overtly, sometimes covertly, until the present time. And that, boys and girls, is what we call the "patriarchy."

Patriarchy

Yes, it's a real thing. It's a word that gets thrown around a lot these days. Most of the time, it seems to just mean anything men do that women don't like.

Sometimes it gets applied to things that don't make sense—like "manspreading." If you don't know what "manspreading" is, it describes how men take up a lot of space with their arms over chairs or their legs spread apart. (Men tell me it's to ensure air circulation down south because, apparently, things can get sweaty down there.) Women who have a bone to pick with men call this an example of patriarchy. It seems to be more an example of penis-archy.

Despite how much "patriarchy" gets misused, it is an accurate word for the patterns of male dominance that came into being after the garden.

Many people (men and women both) don't believe in patriarchy at this point. We've thrown the word around so much it's kind of like the boy who cried wolf, but it isn't a political fairytale. Even though I have been told by many women (usually ultraconservative ladies who married and stayed married to their childhood sweethearts) that they have *never* experienced any kind of oppression or repression at the hands of any male counterparts, the imbalance of power is very real.

The truth is, there is not a woman reading this book who has not experienced the effects of this imbalance, whether they realize it or not. Oftentimes, it's not intentional or malicious. It's just the way boys and girls have been taught to interact in this fallen world order.

We've all known, to some degree, men who have misused their strength and/or their authority over us, knowingly or unknowingly. Whether that's a father or father figure, an ex-husband (I call them "wasbands"), an ex-lover, a brother, an uncle, a cousin, a boss, a pastor, or perhaps a perfect stranger. The aftereffects of this misuse of male power are why so many women have difficulty expressing their femininity and embracing their natural design.

The feminine is inherently strong, yet soft, but some women don't want to be soft. They want to be hard. They despise the empathy and kindness of the authentic feminine because it has allowed them to be taken advantage of too many times.

Hell Hath No Fury…

Modern media glorifies the archetype of a woman who is aggressive, kicking ass and taking names, strong, promiscuous, and who doesn't need anyone. We celebrate these fictional protagonists because we wish we could be like them. We wish we could be strong like Annalise Keating, Olivia Pope, Diana Prince, Lara Croft, Captain Marvel, or Miranda Priestly in the movies and TV shows we adore because we're tired of being the "weaker sex."

We want to be the ice queen—beautiful, untouchable, strong, and powerful. We don't want to be broken, so we try to be unbreakable. We cover our hearts in titanium plating and post a big "Keep Out" sign. We never let people get close to us, truly close to us, because that's how we've been hurt in the past or how we've seen our mothers, sisters, or female friends hurt before us.

Maybe you were sexually, emotionally, physically, and/ or verbally abused, and now you're waging war on your feminine form because it's brought pain into your life. You associate being a girl with being dismissed, ignored, devalued, hurt, abused, raped, and/or oppressed. I know at times it can feel like it's unsafe to be a girl.

I'm the mother of two daughters and I remember sitting down with them and having "the talk." No, not the "where babies come from" talk, but the "what you have to do to survive in this world as a girl" talk. Be friendly, but not too friendly. Park in well-lit areas. Make sure someone always knows where you're going. Make sure the doors are locked when you're home alone. Don't go anywhere by yourself, and certainly don't ever, ever walk down a street by yourself after dark. It's an unfortunate, but absolutely necessary, talk that all women must have with the younger women they love.

Sex as a Superpower

Women and children have been preyed upon in the global culture for centuries, including in the "modern" United States. In fact, women's bodies and sexuality have become such a commodity that many women have become desensitized and are able to give their bodies sexually without a second thought. They think that is what they need to do to get what they want. To them, it's the way to obtain power and control for the purpose of safety and security in relationships and sometimes even in business or their career. That sounds more sinister and premeditated than it looks in everyday life. It might just look like sleeping with your boyfriend because you've been taught that is what is going to get him to finally propose; buying the booty shorts (or, as I call them, "denim underwear") for your preteen daughter because you want her to be popular; or going along with a boss's sexual harassment because you want to be successful in your career. The majority of women have been programmed to believe that their sexuality is their intrinsic value, and they will barter and trade that value to get what they think they most want and need.

> The majority of women have been programmed to believe that their sexuality is their intrinsic value, and they will barter and trade that value to get what they think they most want and need.

This is reinforced in pop culture with iconic songs such as Cardi B's "WAP." This song won the American Music Award and People's Choice Awards for 2020. I was going to include some of the lyrics here, but when I went to look them up, they were so bad, I decided I couldn't do that to you or myself. (You can look them up if you're dying of curiosity. WARNING: They are *very* explicit.) The premise of the song, just like many songs by chart-topping divas such as Madonna, Beyoncé, and Rihanna, perpetuates the idea of using sex as currency to get what you want from men—whether that's commitment, cars, jewelry, or money—all while calling this "empowerment." It's taking what's been weaponized against us, our sexuality, and turning it back around and weaponizing it against men. It was an inevitable pendulum swing, but it's destroying our God-given femininity.

And you know what else is destroying it? Religion.

Purity as a, Well…a Superpower

Popular religious doctrine also reinforces that a woman's value is in her sexuality, or more specifically, her lack of sexuality—her virginity. The most current iteration of this is the purity movement. The modern version of it seems to have mainly started in the 1990s with True Love Waits and the deluge of purity rings, public ceremonies for vows of abstinence, and repression-based sex education.

I met a wonderful young woman, Gwen, on a book tour a few years ago who was so pregnant, she was about ready to pop. Gwen had been a part of the purity movement and had even been a worship leader within the movement. She'd had a purity ring, taken the vows, done the ceremonies, and even led other people through it, only to wind up pregnant out of wedlock herself after a consensual encounter with a coworker.

What went wrong? (Well, besides all the weird cultish rituals we just described.) Gwen had a secret hiding in her heart that, like a ticking time bomb, blew the whole thing up. It was the same sad secret one in four girls under the age of eighteen carries with them every day. Gwen had been sexually abused and had never told anyone. As her well-meaning family and spiritual community were pushing her into vows of chastity and the people around her were talking about how bad sex outside marriage was, Gwen was silently suffering in shame, feeling like a purity imposter.

There are hundreds of thousands of girls whose sexual innocence has already been taken against their will, others who made a decision in the heat of the moment, and a growing majority who have been abused by exposure to pornography or other explicit media. For these girls, the emphasis on "purity" is more traumatizing and retraumatizing than it is healing and redemptive. This avoidant philosophy along the lines of the movie *Eternal Sunshine of the Spotless Mind* teaches us that sex is bad, bad, bad—until it's expected to be magically good the instant you say "I do."

God wants to show you that your value is intrinsic. It cannot be diminished by anything, because your value is not in your vagina—it's in your feminine heart.

This philosophy completely disregards the reality of our hypersexualized culture and heaps shame on our young people for every sexual thought and feeling instead of teaching them how to interact with their sexuality in a healthy way. In my opinion, it is the root cause of the rising sexual promiscuity, dysfunction, and deviance in our culture today.

God wants to change all that. He wants you to know your value as a woman and as a wife is not in your body, your physical appearance, your ability to have children, or your ability to keep up with the Kardashians.

He wants to show you that your value is intrinsic. It cannot be diminished by anything, because your value is not in your vagina—it's in your feminine heart.

Chapter Four

Reunited and It Feels So Good

*I*think after everything you've just read, you can under-stand why this subject is such a hotbed of controversy. You don't just have "relationship problems." Men and women everywhere have been having problems connecting for thousands of years. Of course there's a battle going on inside of you. You literally have centuries worth of bad infor-mation influencing your views of yourself, men, marriage, and even God. This bad information is even backed up by a lot of corroborating evidence not just by history but by your own bad experiences too.

> We can choose to lie in the marriage bed that Jesus made.

If you're looking at history, it will tell you that men and women will attract as oppo-sites do, but they don't cohab-itate. In our counterfeit identi-ties, we absolutely don't. If you look only at the facts, you will come to the conclusion that men and women can never live in harmony.

Thank God that his truth is greater than any fact. The truth is that we have been created for one another, and when we have healed and healthy hearts, we make an amazing team.

The Ministry of "Re"

Since the finished work of the cross, we no longer have to lie in the marriage bed that Adam and Eve's sin made. We can choose to lie in the marriage bed that Jesus made. We as a people are destined to be the bride of Christ, and we as women are created to be the bride of man. We can have good, healthy relationships with one another but only under the ministry of reconciliation.

It's true the curse separated us, but the cross reunites us. In other words, we cannot have healthy relationships outside Jesus, so we *need* to stop trying. We've seen in the prior chapter how people tried, and it didn't work. That's not just about romance. That includes family, friends, and even your relationship with yourself.

The fall of mankind brought "dis," but the cross brought "re"—restoration, reconciliation, revival, repentance, reunion, regeneration, and relationship.

You were created to live in abundance in every area of your life and this area is no different. I know you're frustrated with your love life. (Why else would you be reading this book?) At this point, I hope you can see that this problem isn't your problem. Your problem areas are the places where you have the most unhealed wounds. These unhealed wounds are harboring fears, lies, and false narratives that create havoc in your life as they mature and manifest through emotions such as guilt, shame, unworthiness, and fear. These are powerful emotions that can begin to lead to all kinds of painful behaviors, which are the "problems."

> Your problem areas are the places where you have the most unhealed wounds.

These problems can make you feel like you're walking in a circle, like you're living the same sad story over and over again in a relentless, never-ending *Groundhog Day* marathon—different day, same bullcrap. You think you're making headway, but then you wake up and you're right back at the same dang place in that same chair in the waiting room, holding the number 144. It's enough to make anyone give up. You've been disappointed so many times that you don't even want to get your hopes up again.

That's why you need someone to get their hopes up for you and help you grab ahold of what's always been yours from the very beginning.

Get Out of the Waiting Room

Several months ago, I went to an event to hear a well-known speaker. If I'm being honest, I didn't really want to go because I knew it was going to be crowded, and I knew the venue was small. But my three adult children convinced me that it would be a mistake to miss out on such a great opportunity. It's amazing how persuasive adult children can be. They are even more persuasive than toddlers when they really want something; plus, they have better negotiation skills. Since it's a miracle if your kids even want you to hang out with them after they turn eighteen, I decided I better go. I got there fairly early, but there was already a long line and having been to this venue before, I wondered if we would be able to get a seat.

As the sweat trickled down my entire body (because Texas is hot as Hell's front porch, y'all), I started to feel less and less convinced that this was a quality decision and hoped that we wouldn't be able to stay. So as you can see, I was not that invested in this opportunity. Maybe I get in, maybe I don't. Maybe I get to go home and strip down naked in the air conditioning.

As I'm thinking about how nice that sounded, the line starts moving a little bit and I heard a woman's voice behind me. She was talking at a decibel level that, when I was a kid, adults called our "outside voice." Which I guess was okay since we did happen to be outside. I could just imagine as I listened to her rattle on that she had probably been told a million times that she was being too loud. "It's not ladylike to be so loud," "You need to lower your voice," and "People are staring." I didn't care at all that she was being loud, but it was even more pronounced since the majority of other people in line were waiting patiently and quietly, likely to conserve energy because it was just that hot.

I began to listen more closely, and from what I could gather, she was super excited because she loved this special speaker. I nonchalantly turned around to see her, just to see who was talking. The people around her seemed amused and kind of like "who is this person?" It was clear she was there alone and was so excited she was gushing to complete strangers.

As we all listened to her go on and on enthusiastically, we learned that she had been following this speaker and watching him on television for fifteen years and had always wanted to see him in person, but she had never had the chance. She was just beside herself with excitement.

I remember thinking in my mind, *Oh that's nice. I'm really happy for this lady.* Right about then, the doors opened, and the line began to move.

By the time I got inside the venue, there was not an empty seat in sight. Ushers were already telling people that there was an overflow room for those of us who couldn't find a seat in the main auditorium. If you don't know what an overflow room is, it's an auxiliary room where you can watch the event on a screen.

I can watch TV at home, naked, and in the air conditioning, I thought to myself. "Hey, if we can't find a seat, let's just go home," I whispered to my husband and son.

I looked around for my daughters, and they were already seated with friends who had been saving seats for them, so I motioned to them that we were just going to leave. They frowned and nodded, showing they were sad but understood.

As my husband, my son, and I were walking out, I felt prompted to turn one last time and walk up the aisle. And so I did. I stopped, turned around, went up the aisle, and there were three empty seats. I asked the guy that was sitting next to them if these seats were really empty and he said yes, they were.

I couldn't believe it. Three empty seats were in plain sight. I motioned to my husband and son and they came over. We sat down and waited for the event to start.

The pre-event was playing and the screen message indicated we had thirty minutes until the main attraction, so I decided to grab a quick bathroom break.

While I was in the stall, I heard someone come in distraught. They started crying and started talking to someone about how disappointed they were that they didn't get into the main auditorium.

I recognized that voice. It was the woman from the line who, just fifteen minutes earlier, had been on Cloud Nine thinking that her dream was about to come true.

Does this sound like your love life? You think you've found someone with real potential, someone who could finally be your magic bullet of happiness. You think you're cresting the peak of relationship bliss, but it doesn't happen, and you end up crying alone in your bathtub yet again.

Back to my story.

Because what she had wanted to happen had not happened, this lady had adopted a different story. It wasn't a new story based on truth. It was an old story based on negative past experiences. This story was about how she was always a day late and a dollar short. You know—always in coach when everyone else is in first class. Not being able to find a seat in the main room brought all the lies that she believed about herself to the surface, including, "I knew this would happen to me. I'm always left out. I've been watching him on TV for fifteen years and now I have to go do it again because they put me in the overflow room. I don't want to watch him on a screen. I wanted to see him in person."

My heart broke for her because even though this was just about a speaker and an event, I knew this was the main theme of her entire life. How did I know? That used to be the main theme of my life too.

I didn't say a word to her; I just quietly washed my hands and went back into the auditorium determined to find this woman a seat.

I was on a mission. There had to be a seat in here for this lady. We tend to find what we are expecting to find, and because I was looking for a seat through eyes of hope and expectancy, I found one.

I asked the person sitting next to it if the seat was empty, and yes, it was. So I put my water bottle on it to save it, and I went to the waiting room where this lady was sitting. I was so excited to tell her that I had found her a seat. I was imagining in my mind how thankful and happy she was going to be.

But when I went into the waiting room, to my surprise, she wasn't alone. She had two littles with her.

I wasn't expecting this. I hadn't seen them waiting with her in line and I was trying to decide what to do next when she looked right at me. I said to her, "Hey, I just wanted to let you know I heard you in line talking about how excited you were to hear this speaker, and then I heard you in the bathroom talking about how disappointed you were to be in the overflow. I found you a seat, but I didn't realize you had two children with you, so I'm going to go look for a seat for all of you and then I'll be back."

She wasn't optimistic at all. She said, "Oh, yeah, it's completely packed in there. There are no seats for us. But thanks anyway." She'd already given up. While she may have been able to believe that there was one seat for her, she definitely didn't believe that there was room for her and her children too.

After all, this is what always happened to her. She was used to this narrative. She believed she had to settle, couldn't have what she wanted, and that nothing ever worked out for her. She believed that was "just her life."

I would not be deterred. I knew that she was there to receive the desire of her heart. I went back into the main auditorium, and I looked around for three seats. I was looking everywhere. I was asking people if seats were taken. I had complete faith that there was space for this woman and her children somewhere in the room.

Right then, I saw my daughters motioning to different seats. "Hey, come sit with us!" they said.

"What do you mean?" I asked.

"The people who were sitting here are gone," they said. "There are four empty seats with us."

So my husband, son, and I moved up to those seats and we saved the three seats we had been sitting in. Three seats—that was all this woman needed. I went back into the waiting room where I found the woman and her children. They were able to come into the place where they had always belonged.

But that's not where the story ends. Because as I was basking in the afterglow of helping this woman receive what God had for her, I overheard an usher telling someone that in her haste to help others find their seats, she had forgotten to save herself a seat.

"Now I don't have anywhere to sit," she said sadly. "I'm going to have to go into the other room."

So I interrupted and said to her, "Hey, three rows up from here on the end there's an empty seat with a water bottle. That's my water bottle, and that seat is open."

She was so excited and she was able to go up and sit in that seat I had originally found for the other woman, but it was actually meant for this usher instead.

At this point, it sounds like I'm an eavesdropper, doesn't it? But I believe that God allowed me to supernaturally overhear both these conversations so he could teach me (and you) some powerful lessons about the way he works.

First, God will send people into your life to believe for you when you've given up. Also, the blind spots created by our past disappointments are keeping us from seeing the blessing that's right in front of us. Last, we need to believe God is sending people to help us. God has sent me to help you just like he sent me to help that woman. He has sent me to help you receive what he already has for you. Those seats already belonged to that woman. They already had her name on them. She just needed someone to believe when she had stopped believing. She needed someone to help her get her expectations back up because she had been disappointed too many times.

But then the usher situation is just as important. Sometimes we get so damaged and so disappointed that all we can see is ourselves and what we want but don't have. We've got to look at others. Because when we're busy helping other people and not feeling sorry for ourselves, what we help make happen for others, God will do for us.

Now let's apply these lessons to our love lives.

Both of these ladies were willing to sit in the waiting room because they believed God had good things for everyone else, but not them. There are many reasons people feel this way, but you can't let them hold you back from the good plans God has for you.

Chapter Five

Life Is Hard
When Our
Hearts Are Hard

*E*ven if we don't come out of the box this way, believing that life is just one big ride on the struggle bus, most of us get there pretty quickly. Some of us get there even before we're out of diapers. That's my story. Some people inherit money, property, and businesses from their family. I inherited trauma. Have you ever seen those National Geographic documentaries about the wild animal kingdom? You know the ones, right?

They are narrated by a person speaking in a monotone, and yet somehow it's a very dramatic voice telling us what we never wanted to know about the circle of life. In every documentary, there's a mother giraffe, gazelle, or elephant trying to give birth to her offspring. Meanwhile, lurking nearby in the tall grass, there always seems to be a pride of hungry lions, jackals, hyenas, or some other kind of predator just looking for a tasty snack. Every time I see one of those documentaries, I feel as if I'm listening to the narration of my childhood.

> Some people inherit money, property, and businesses from their family. I inherited trauma.

The narrator's voice lets us know that the baby has been born, but right before we get a chance to admire the squishy newborn that just plopped out of its mother's backside, mom is already kicking it saying, "Get up, baby. You gotta get *moving!*"

The entire herd also senses the danger that surrounds them, and they go into full-blown panic mode. This adorable little nugget doesn't have time to be a baby; it's been alive for less than fifteen minutes and it's already in danger. It has to start running for its life immediately. That was me. I came out of my mother's womb running for my life.

My entire lineage lived their lives in a never-ending, unrelenting fear response. I was born into a place that felt unsafe, inhabited by broken and unsafe people. Everywhere you looked as far as the eye could see, there were only broken relationships, broken promises, and broken hearts. In fact, for the majority of my life, I had no idea there was another kind of heart except a broken heart.

This is how we start believing life is hard; it is because our broken hearts are hard. When something becomes wounded repetitively, it develops a callus. It's the body's self-defense mechanism against that repeated trauma. Think about your feet in a new pair of sandals. If those new shoes rub your toe the wrong way, over and over again, it creates a wound. That wound hurts at first but eventually that area will form a thicker skin, a hardened shell to keep it safe from being hurt anymore.

Maybe the lies you believe about love and marriage didn't originate in childhood like mine did, but they originated somewhere. In one way or another our hearts get broken, and without exception everyone suffers in this life. But the effects of those incidents don't end when the immediate suffering ends or when the traumatic event is considered to be over. Many times the effects of those experiences stay with us for a lifetime or even, in some cases like mine, for generations. It's important for you to understand that trauma doesn't just hurt us, it creates different versions of us.

That thing you went through that almost killed you? It's still trying. It's trying to kill your destiny and dreams, your hope and your future. These sad events in our lives or in the lives of the people who came before us, all the way back to the garden, alter us just like the shoe alters the toe. They harden us, change our shape, and sabotage our original design. Sometimes the change is sudden and dramatic like someone who has post-traumatic stress disorder (also known as broken heart syndrome) because of a catastrophic event in their lives. It might have been the death of a child or spouse, an infidelity, a vicious assault, a betrayal, or any other kind of tragic or unexpected event. Something so brutal it leaves us in the kind of pain that forces us to fragment in order just to face tomorrow.

> Trauma doesn't just hurt us, it creates different versions of us.

But in most cases, the personality change is more subtle and gradual over time. These false personalities slowly gain traction because of little trauma after little trauma, and then one big heartbreak and several more little disappointments. Pretty soon you have layer after layer of trauma-created identity fueled by faulty belief systems, and you don't even know it.

*Don't you know that when you allow
even a little lie into your heart, it can
permeate your entire belief system?*
—GALATIANS 5:9 TPT

By the time we reach our 30s and older, this counter-feit personality becomes ingrained and very much in charge of our daily lives. It is picking out your clothes, eating your breakfast in the morning, and getting ready to go to a job it chose (which the real you hates). When it comes to your love life it is the one that is swiping right on those dating apps or smiling back at that guy across the room.

It's the one with social anxiety who claims she's an "introvert," but at the same time feels crippled by loneliness. It's the same person who prides herself on "telling it like it is," but who loses friends because "they just can't handle the truth."

We will often defend these false personalities to the death when they're causing us pain, saying, "This is just who I am!" We will say this even when they're costing us rela-tionships, opportunities, and dreams.

People will blame their Myers-Briggs type, their Enneagram number, or their zodiac sign (if they're into that) for their unhealthy behaviors and patterns. We blame them for our limitations and the current state of the life we don't love, pretending that things will never change because we were "born this way."

These personalities are *not* the real us. They tend to vacillate somewhere between victim and survivor, but no matter what version you gravitate toward, the Bible tells us these brokenhearted identities cannot be trusted.

This is what the Bible says about your broken heart:

. . . is dark and deceitful, a puzzle that no one
can figure out. But I, God, search the heart
and examine the mind. I get to the heart of the
human. I get to the root of things. I treat them
as they really are, not as they pretend to be.

—JEREMIAH 17: 9-10 MSG

Does that sound like someone you want at the wheel of your car? These different versions of us with their broken hearts are dangerous. Those traumas that created them might not have killed you, but they are still trying to, through the lies you now believe because of them. Those lies create blind spots and filters.

Did you know that 94 percent of fatal car accidents are caused by some kind of blind spot and human error?[2] The driver made a fatal mistake because they could not see something they needed to see until it was too late.

When we are navigating our lives, including our love lives, blinded by all these lies, we can't see things, people, or situations the way they really are. We only see things the way we are inside, through the dirty lens of our past experiences and the way we've interpreted those experiences.

We compensate for blind spots in two ways—being overly reckless (Victim) or being overly cautious (Survivor). Most people vacillate somewhere within that spectrum or with some combination of the two. We can also be a Victim in one area of our lives and be a Survivor in another.

When we are in a counterfeit Victim mode it looks as if we're being unaccountable and making bad decisions regardless of who it hurts. We expect others to solve our problems or clean up our messes. We are self-destructive and yet constantly blame other people for the consequences of our poor choices.

In other words, you know you can't see clearly, but you don't care. You're gonna follow your heart anyway.

I often see posters and bumper stickers that read, "Follow Your Heart." I answer under my breath, "Not unless you want to end up in a ditch."

The Victim mindset says, "I don't have to make wise decisions or look out for anybody else. Everybody should just get out of my way. I've been through too much already. I'm owed this."

The Victim mentality is not only caused by trauma, it creates new trauma as our reckless decisions and risky behaviors have bad consequences in our lives and the lives of others. The Victim has no boundaries. They do whatever feels good at the moment. They ignore obvious danger signs in relationships. They are the ones who trust their feelings above all else including any sound advice from other voices in their lives.

Here's an example: Taylor has a long history of dysfunctional dating. She has been in relationship after relationship with men who, after a short amount of time, show themselves to be abusive. Every relationship starts out the same— fast and furious chemistry, magnetic attraction, quickly "falling in love," romantic dinners, flowers, immediate escalation into pet names, and physical intimacy. This fairytale quickly turns into a nightmare.

One day, Taylor's posting videos and romantic selfies with her latest guy on Facebook saying how much she loves him. The next, she changes her Facebook status to "single" and blocks and deletes him; in some cases, these relationships even end in a restraining order or worse.

> You keep trying again and again with no new information, speeding through life, hurting yourself, hurting others, and going nowhere fast.

You can't trust a heart with a Victim lens. You can't listen to it. You can't follow its deepest hopes and desires until it's regenerated. Until then, it's sure to leave you swerving your car into the other lane. It doesn't matter if there's something there already, you're just crossing your fingers, closing your eyes, and hoping it works out. You're not gonna wait, you're in a hurry, you're lonely, you want what you want, and you want it now. You don't have any respect for yourself or others, and it shows. Your car has all kinds of dings and dents from past accidents, all your previous bad decisions, breakups, and breakdowns. You keep trying again and again with no new information, speeding through life, hurting yourself, hurting others, and going nowhere fast. The song playing on your radio is "Love Hurts" and for you, it definitely does.

When we are in that opposite counterfeit on the spectrum, the Survivor personality, it looks a bit different and less dramatic, but it's just as detrimental to our love lives. Survivor personalities are driving their little electric cars forty-five miles an hour in the fast lane. That's as fast as their cars can go because they don't want to drive those fast fuel-powered engines anymore. Nope, too dangerous. Slow and steady wins the race. The only pace they're comfortable with is a snail's pace. They have their hazard lights on, giving the stink eye to anyone who even thinks about coming near their lane. They're blowing the horn constantly. *Don't get close to me! I see you trying to come near me. Stay away!* Their mantra is, "Fool me once, shame on you. Fool me twice, shame on me."

Here's an example: Sharon has been to years of counseling to recover from her divorce. She is what I call over-counseled. She prides herself on being self-aware, self-actualized, and has all her ducks in a row (or does she?). Sharon has become very controlling in an effort to keep herself safe, but she wouldn't call herself that. She'd call herself "responsible," which, for Sharon and others like her, is just a fancy word for "afraid."

Sharon's always looking for the first sign of imperfection and is on high alert. To her, every flag is a red flag because that's all she's looking for. It's like when I needed a red dress for an event. I logged on to all the websites that sold dresses and I set the search filters to only show red dresses. Because of that, red dresses were all I could see. When you're in Survivor mode, you're only on the lookout for trouble or danger, and because of that, that's all you see.

Sharon thinks this is having "good boundaries." She's constantly in a state of flux, frantically searching for a chink in a guy's armor. No matter how genuine and amazing a guy is, she's always thinking he's too good to be true so he must be hiding something, and *I'm gonna find it.*

Sharon doesn't blame other people for things that go wrong in her life. She blames herself. She takes full responsibility for "choosing the wrong guy" in her past relationships and will *never* let that happen again. As a result, she doesn't trust herself to choose at all and when love shows up, she finds something wrong with it every time.

Both Victim and Survivor modes will keep us stuck and hold us back from the life we really want, if we let them. I don't know about you, but I don't want these counterfeit chicks choosing anything for me anymore. That broken-hearted identity had me on a crazy wild goose chase for most of my life trying to give her what she wanted to feel safe, secure, and whole again, but nothing seemed to work. This identity will have you chasing shadows and living a life that's completely unworthy of you and your true destiny if you continue to let it take the lead.

For example, when I was a young, hurting, and confused girl, my broken heart led me smack-dab into a self-made love story that was wrong for me, wrong for him, and threatened both of our mental, emotional, spiritual, and even physical health before we finally had no choice but to call it quits. Leaving that marriage was one of the hardest decisions of my life. It was what I call a "double bind," meaning I was stuck both ways by some type of belief I had in my heart that was keeping me in limbo and unable to make a decision. You might be familiar with the saying "you're damned if you do, and you're damned if you don't." This is what that saying means. It feels like you're being torn apart because neither decision is what you really want, and so you stay stuck forever.

Chapter Six

It's Time to
Get Unstuck

*N*obody says, "When I grow up, I want to be divorced," but I got married young without an ounce of good information on what marriage or love looked like. I was in no position to make a lifelong commitment to anyone. But do you think I let that stop me? Of course not! My heart would not settle for anything less than marrying this man. The problem was, he didn't want to marry me. In fact, every time we got into a relationship, we fought and broke up. He was willing to move on, but I was too afraid to let the "dream" go. It was obvious to everyone that we were a bad match, except to my poor, little, deceived heart. I would have begged, borrowed, and stolen to get him to love me, and I practically did. I was sure I couldn't live without him. Years later, my healing heart realized I couldn't live *with* him.

> My little twenty-year-old counterfeit self raced to the altar on that hot June afternoon past more red flags than the Daytona 500.

I finally won. I got that ring on my finger through much manipulation, scheming, and outright pretending to be what he wanted. I didn't know I was pretending; I just thought I could be anything he wanted me to be because I "loved him so much." My little twenty-year-old counterfeit self raced to the altar on that hot June afternoon past more red flags than the Daytona 500.

I was wearing a dress that didn't fit. I was surrounded by people I hardly knew, running toward a young man who had no idea what he was getting himself into. All I cared about was filling that God-shaped hole inside my chest. I didn't know it was a God-shaped hole; I didn't know God. I had heard about Jesus since I was little, and I thought that sounded like a fun fairytale. I was thinking about looking into it, I really was, but not right now. Right now, I needed something with a pulse that had some skin on it to fit in that dang hole. I needed what I thought was stability and security.

You see, I thought it was a man-shaped hole because I had watched all the women I knew growing up run after a man to make them feel safe, loved, and valuable. They would stick man after man into that hole inside their own lying hearts trying to find the one that fit just right.

So I did the same. I found a cute, tall, talented man and I did my best to stuff him into that hole in my heart. I recognized my mistake just two days into my honeymoon when I woke up and realized the hole was still there; instead of being filled, it had gotten even bigger. Year after year with every argument, every harsh word, every rejection, it got bigger and bigger until eventually it threatened to swallow me alive. I could have left. I didn't have any religious convictions holding me there, at least not yet. I hadn't even had my spiritual awakening, but God or no God, my stubborn heart would be darned if I was gonna be divorced just like the rest of my messed-up family. I was gonna make it work, even if I had to keep up that false identity for the rest of my life, even if it killed me—and several times it almost did.

I know many of you can relate. You've experienced divorce, you've experienced an abusive marriage, or at the very least, like me, an immature and destructive relationship where you began to believe more things about yourself that were not true. Things such as you're unworthy, you're insignificant, you're not lovable. And those ideas continue to be reinforced and take you lower and lower into that place of false identity.

My divorce wasn't a divorce—it was a rescue mission.

I believe that, sometimes, God looks at us and says, "I can't leave you here, because if I do, you're going to die. You're drowning and this other person either can't or won't pull you up, so I'm going to have to pull you out before you go under."

Nobody Puts Baby in a Corner but Baby

God intervened in my situation and yours before there was a spiritual, emotional, mental, or maybe even physical death.

But even after I was released from that situation, it didn't stop me from disqualifying myself. Subconsciously, I believed I was disqualified from ever stepping into another love story. Even though God wasn't punishing me, it didn't matter because I was punishing myself.

Failure doesn't rob us of potential but it does rob us of confidence.

I know we all love that movie quote, "Nobody puts Baby in the corner." But sometimes Baby puts Baby in the corner all day long and twice on Sundays.

I was sticking myself in the corner. I was putting myself in time-out. I was putting myself back in the waiting room, and who knows how long I would have let myself stay there before I would have allowed myself to be "qualified" enough to have another chance.

That might be where you are too. You've put yourself in time-out. You're punishing yourself. You picked the wrong man, and now you're damaged goods. You're divorced, you're a single mom, you have a sexually transmitted disease, you're left behind when all your girlfriends seem happily married.

Some of you have been in this waiting room more than once, even more than twice. Just as soon as you think you learned your lesson and you give yourself another chance, you do the same thing all over again. Right when your number is about to be called, something happens that you think puts you right back at the end of line.

> I know we all love that movie quote, "Nobody puts Baby in the corner." But sometimes Baby puts Baby in the corner all day long and twice on Sundays.

For instance, I have several beautiful, amazing women in my mentorship groups who have serious health problems. It would be really easy for them to say, "Nope, I don't get a love story." And a lot of people would agree with them. They'd be like, "Yeah, this is too complicated now; you better wait until you have that figured out." They would put themselves back into that familiar holding pattern just waiting for the day when everything is perfect.

God hasn't put them at the end of the line, and he also hasn't pressed pause on their love story waiting for them to get it all together. He hasn't put you in those places, either, but we put ourselves there. I did that.

On my very first date with my now-husband, instead of showing up to that cafe excited and full of anticipation, I showed up full of fear and armed with all the reasons this was a bad idea. Reasons such as: I had a mental illness, undiagnosed physical ailments, I wasn't ready, not worthy of any kind of romance or love story, and he should definitely run while he had the chance. While you might be thinking I'm being dramatic, I sat down and shared with him all the reasons dating me was a bad idea. I literally came close to yelling, "Run, Forrest!"

You might not have done this as overtly as I did, but here are some "reasons" we put ourselves on hold without even realizing it. One of these might be why you're still waiting instead of dating the man of your dreams. Read through this list and see if any of these look familiar:

I'm disqualified.

- Divorced
- Single mom
- Too old
- Missed the boat
- Have a sexually transmitted disease
- Overweight
- Handicapped
- Infertile/unable to have children
- Have debt
- Have been diagnosed with a mental illness
- Being punished by God
- Health problems

I'm fine being single.

- If it were going to happen, it would have happened by now.
- I don't want a man to mess up my life.
- I have a "good" life.
- Jesus is my husband/God should be enough me.
- God must not want this for me.
- It's easier to be alone.

Waiting is good!

- I'm not ready.
- "Good things come to those who wait."
- I don't want to pick the wrong guy.
- It will happen when God wants it to happen.
- It's biblical to wait.
- It's not God's time yet.

Waiting Rooms, Preparation
Rooms, and Birthing Rooms

There's something very important you need to know—in the Kingdom of God, there are no waiting rooms. There are only preparation rooms and birthing rooms. Nowhere in the Bible does God tell you to sit down and wait without having something to do on your end.

We like to quote Isaiah 40 to justify the "I'm just waiting on God" mentality, but that's a misinterpretation of that verse.

But those who wait upon GOD get fresh strength.
They spread their wings and soar like eagles,
They run and don't get tired, they
walk and don't lag behind.

—Isaiah 40:31 MSG

The word that's translated as "wait" actually means "expectantly prepare" in the original Hebrew. Every time God gives us a promise, he's really giving us a process. It's an invitation to prepare for the fruition of the deepest desires of our heart.

I saw a really weird documentary once; I don't know if any of you saw it. I think it was on The History Channel. But it was about women who showed up at the emergency room and didn't even know they were pregnant.

I'm just going to go ahead and leave that there for a second.

I know what you're thinking. How is that even possible? How can you *not* know that you are nine months pregnant? It just seems crazy, right?

Immediately, I thought, *Okay, there's got to be something else going on here.* But it was an interesting documentary because babies are a blessing, right? Most of these people were happy to find out they were giving birth because first they thought they were dying, so that's a relief, and secondly because something new was about to be born.

> In the Kingdom of God, there are no waiting rooms. There are only preparation rooms and birthing rooms.

At the same time, they weren't ready for these babies. What I saw in this documentary was that, while this event was amazing, incredible, and supernatural, their lives didn't have room for a baby. How silly would it be if you found out you were pregnant and you sat in the waiting room of your doctor's office until it was time to give birth.

I'm sure the nurses would ask you, "Excuse me, what are you doing?"

"Oh, I'm just waiting for my baby."

It would be just as ridiculous if you left your doctor's office and told yourself that the doctor is wrong, that there's no way you could be pregnant, and went on with your life as if nothing had happened.

The correct response to finding out you're pregnant is *preparation*. I believe you are like this, pregnant with a promise from God for a world-changing marriage. But where there is a promise, there is also a process. It's time to stop waiting and start preparing.

Nelson Mandela said we won't prepare for anything we don't really believe is going to happen. Do you believe marriage is going to happen? If you do, you need to start preparing, because the proof of belief is preparation.

The first thing you need to do to prepare is to go after all the things you believe have been keeping you doubting that marriage will ever happen for you. Doubt is just uncertainty, which causes inaction; it is time to get to the root of doubt because it has already kept you waiting far too long. God wants to take you off pause and hit the play button on your love life, but you have to do your part to help him.

> The proof of belief is preparation.

Chapter Seven

Getting Out of Your Own Way

Y ou're a liar and so am I.

Without exception everyone believes and is telling themselves (and others) at least one lie right now. Most people are telling themselves and others a LOT of lies. Broken hearts have turned even the most honest person into a habitual liar. How is that possible?

It's possible because the traumas that broke your heart and created different versions of you came as a complete package, lies included. They often show up as areas where we describe ourselves as "stuck." Areas of confusion and hopelessness, knowing that there's more, but not knowing how to get it. Original trauma is not the biggest threat to your happiness. It's not what's going to prevent you from living the epic love story that God has written in the Story of You. It's the *lies* you believe because of that trauma that will, and the false identity that those lies are reinforcing.

In other words, we're not stuck on the outside, we're stuck on the inside.

Kate came to me in the summer of 2020. She'd already been married twice. In her first marriage, she got married young, had two children, realized it was an abusive situation, and got out.

Unfortunately, like many divorcees, her former husband had visitation rights to their children. That wasn't something that was in Kate's control to prevent. While he wasn't abusive to the children, there was some evidence of neglect during visitation times at his home. Kate was uncomfortable with the children going to their dad's, but because she didn't know what to do, she ignored her misgivings.

One weekend while Kate's former husband was working a third shift at his place of work, his family member was at the house staying with the children. The family member heard Kate's 15-month-old son crying that night but didn't go to check on him. That family member did not want to be bothered and thought the child was just being cranky and didn't want to go to sleep.

The 15-month-old wasn't cranky; he was in distress. Later that night, he died.

I think we can all agree that this is one of the worst kinds of trauma. As a mother, it makes me emotional just thinking about it. At the time I met Kate, this tragedy had happened many years earlier but she was still stuck.

Why? Because even though the trauma was far in the past, it had created a counterfeit version of Kate called "the bad mother." The lies Kate believed because of this tragedy were still reinforcing that false identity every day. She told herself lies such as, "I shouldn't have let my children go. I should have been there. I should have saved him. I failed him. If I had done my job, he would still be alive. I don't deserve anything good in life anymore."

Almost two decades later, Kate was still beating herself up. She wasn't at fault and she didn't go to prison, but she put herself in a prison. She put herself in "heart jail" as punishment. Because of what she believed about herself, she wasn't able to believe that she deserved anything good.

So what did Kate do? She got married again under the influence of all these lies. Because she was still punishing herself, she was unable to connect in her second marriage.

And despite having two more children with her second husband, that marriage eventually ended in divorce as well.

When I met Kate, her second husband had remarried and now she was back in a situation where visitation from an ex-spouse was occurring. She was once again being forced by a court order to allow her children to be cared for by people outside her home.

Part of the consequences of the lie Kate believed was that she couldn't let her children out of her sight. She had to be a helicopter mom, a smother mother. Anytime her children were with anyone but Kate, she felt as if they weren't safe. So she spent 100 percent of her time making sure nothing bad happened to her remaining children.

I think many of us can say that we would feel the same way for a certain amount of time, but this was fifteen years later. Kate was paralyzed. Every time she would try to step forward and allow the children to spend more time with their dad, she just couldn't do it. After about six months consulting with me, her second husband announced that he was fed up with Kate's monopoly of the kids, and he was suing for joint custody of their children. She was distraught.

Kate asked me to pray that he would not win his lawsuit and thus not be awarded equal custody.

Because Kate had come to me for the purpose of preparing to be married, I asked her a simple question: "Is he a good dad?"

Kate said, "Yes."

I continued, "Is the environment at his house a good environment?"

"Yeah," she said.

"So what's the problem?" I asked. "You're praying and hoping for a love story, but you spend every waking moment trying to keep your children from any type of harm. You don't have room for anyone else." I said, "I can pray for what you want or I can pray for God's will to be done. I believe God's trying to show you that the lies you're believing aren't true, and that your children are safe even when they're not with you."

Kate agreed, and we prayed for God's will. Even though she was afraid, she was willing to let go of control.

Control is a byproduct of fear. If you're a controlling person (even those of you who say you're not), you're afraid. You don't want any surprises. You want to know everything in advance. That's part of that Survivor personality. You're trying to make sure no one swerves into your lane. You're trying to make sure that what hurt you before will never have a chance to hurt you again.

> You're trying to make sure that what hurt you before will never have a chance to hurt you again.

The judge ruled in favor of Kate's former husband and gave him 50 percent custody. She knew that was what needed to happen and that God was making room in her life for new opportunities, including a love story.

Two weeks later, she met an amazing single dad. They have so much in common and a beautiful budding romance that would not have been possible without revealing and healing the lies she had believed.

Just like Kate, each of us has something we're believing that's keeping us from living in the abundance and overflow God wants us to experience. Hopefully by now you can see how this vicious cycle works.

> *The cycle:*
> - Kate experiences trauma: her son passes away.
> - She believes a lie (I'm a bad mother).
> - She speaks the lie and reinforces it (I should have been there; I failed my son).
> - She becomes the lie (fear-based mothering, controlling, helicopter mom).

We go through a trauma, our hearts are poisoned by lies, we believe those lies, we speak those lies, they become our truth, and eventually our everyday identity and reality is shaped by them. This is how what we believe about ourselves, we become, and our behavior follows that identity.

John 10:10

It's time to unpack the boxes in your heart and get rid of what's in them that is hindering you from living your best life. Most people are not living the John 10:10 promise. You know that piece of ancient prose where Jesus died to give you a life better than your wildest dreams?

A thief has only one thing in mind—he wants to
steal, slaughter, and destroy. But I have come to
give you everything in abundance, more than
you expect—*life in its fullness until you overflow!*

—John 10:10 TPT

Very few people can raise their hands and say they
are living an overflowing life. I think most people feel as
if they're running on empty more times than not. Even if
you have some areas that feel full, that you can describe as
pretty good, there are other areas that you definitely know
need work. There might even be a couple of areas where you
know you're riding on the Hot Mess Express.

Because you picked up this book, I'm guessing your
love life is one of those areas where you feel you're tore up
from the floor up and don't know why. I hope you can see
by now that it's because you're being limited by something
you believe. I can hear you saying right now, "Well, Jackie, I
never went through anything like Kate's story. What could
be keeping me single?"

Foxes. That's what.

There Is Change in the Air

Regardless of what the pattern for romance has been in your
life up until this point, I want you to hear God whispering
to you as you read this book: "Arise, my love, and run away
with me to the higher place. For *now* is your time."

What is that higher place? It's a place of a higher perspective. It's looking at things through a healed, healthy, and whole heart, and not through the dirty lens of hurt and trauma.

---

*Can you not discern this new day of destiny breaking forth around you? The early signs of my purposes and plans are bursting forth. The budding vines of new life are now blooming everywhere. The fragrance of their flowers whispers, "**There is change in the air." Arise, my love, my beautiful companion, and run with me to the higher place. For now is the time to arise and come away with me.** For you are my dove, hidden in the split-open rock. It was I who took you and hid you up high in the secret stairway of the sky. Let me see your radiant face and hear your sweet voice. How beautiful your eyes of worship and lovely your voice in prayer. You must catch the troubling foxes, those sly little foxes that hinder our relationship. For they raid our budding vineyard of love to ruin what I've planted within you. Will you catch them and remove them for me? We will do it together.*

—SONG OF SONGS 2:13-15 TPT (EMPHASIS MINE)

I know most of you ladies are familiar with the Song of Songs (also known as the book of the Bible with the word "breasts" in it). This particular passage is kind of the women's anthem. A love letter from the bridegroom. We're like, "Whoo-hoo! The barrenness of my winter is over. Spring is here!" And for those of you hoping for romance in the barren land of loneliness, "table for one," and dates so horrible they leave you asking your-self, *Did I really shave my legs for this?* you might interpret this as "Hallelujah! It's raining men!"

I've read this scripture a million times—out loud, in ministry, at women's conferences; I even put a part of this chapter on the tag to the miniature bouquets I gave to all the single ladies at my wedding, but I never noticed the foxes before.

You must catch the troubling foxes, those sly little foxes that hinder our relationship. For they raid our budding vine-yard of love to ruin what I've planted within you.

You might be asking, "Foxes? What the what? What are these foxes that the bridegroom is talking about?"

The foxes are those lies you're believing. They could be insecurities, faulty belief systems, blind spots, filters, vows, soul ties, trust issues, prejudices, cultural norms, and stereotypes. They are also trauma-based stories we're telling ourselves about who we are, what men are like, how marriage works, and why we still don't have the love we want. They are stories birthed out of disap-pointment, disillusionment, disconnection, failure, and/ or abandonment.

But these foxes don't even have to be things you think are overtly negative. This passage says that they are sly and even little. There's a saying in America, "sly as a fox." Foxes are deceptive. They're sneaky. They can be so small they fit in a carry-on bag and you would never notice them with all your other baggage.

They might even be cute—pithy little quotes and covert "angry woman" memes about how you don't need a man. I mean, what's wrong with independence? Independence seems super important, right? (Especially now that we've learned the history of men and women that was the catalyst for the feminist movements.) Ideas such as: I don't need a man; I can take care of myself; I am woman, hear me roar! Do any of these sound familiar? "A woman needs a man like a fish needs a bicycle," "We've become the men that our mothers wanted us to marry," or how about, "Marriage is a fine institution, but who wants to be institutionalized?" I've seen those quotes on single women's social media, and I've also seen them as magnets on women's refrigerators. Harmless, right? Possibly even necessary.

After everything women have been through, men are pretty much all falling under the category of guilty until proven innocent. That seems reasonable, and that's the problem.

I've seen foxes at the zoo. They look kind of cute. They're fluffy and have tiny little pawsies. But they have sharp teeth, and any farmer will tell you that just like these passive-aggressive ideologies, while they may seem good at first, they can be very destructive.

We may have allowed foxes into our proverbial vineyard because we don't recognize them since they're coming in the form of beliefs that have been handed down from our family. I had one client who was in her mid-thirties who had never had a relationship. Her family are Romanian immigrants, and they insisted that she date and marry from within their community.

Sadly, there are not a lot of eligible Romanian men in Atlanta, Georgia. This cultural lie was keeping her from love and when she confronted it after a few months of my coaching, she gave herself permission to love outside those parameters despite her family's belief system. When that little fox was caught, romance bloomed quickly.

She met and married the love of her life just six months later.

Foxes Destroy Potential

What does the bridegroom say that these little foxes are doing?

----

*For they **raid** our **budding** vineyard of love*
*to **ruin** what I've **planted within** you.*

They're destroying the potential of this love story God's already written for you before it has even had the chance to blossom, to manifest, to mature, to bear fruit, to fulfill God's promise over your life. Remember that divorce, that failure, that rejection? It didn't rob you of potential—it robbed you of *confidence*. We still have the potential to have this beautiful, God-breathed love story, but we lack the confidence to step back in, to trust again, to love again.

Catching the Foxes

Will you catch them and remove them
for me? We will do it together.

The bridegroom is asking us, "Will you do your part? Will you catch them for me? Do you care that your potential is being devoured and destroyed? Do you want my best for you in this area of your life?"

We are being called to action. God has a part that only he can play, but we have a part that only we can play. That's why the permission that you gave God at the beginning of this book is so vital to your success. You can't do this on your own. If you could, you already would have done it. You can't do God's part, but he also can't do yours.

> You can't do this on your own. If you could, you already would have done it. You can't do God's part, but he also can't do yours.

Are you willing to do your part? Are you willing to do your heart work? Are you willing to take a deeper look at yourself instead of blaming other people for your failed relationships? Are you willing to get down to the roots? Can you admit that there's scarcity in your life, that these buds of love are not blooming? He's asking, "Will you catch them for me?" But then he says, "Never mind, let's catch them together."

And that's his promise right now. There's a grace available if you want it. An enabling power to partner with Heaven to break free from everything that's holding you back. The Holy Spirit is standing by, ready to help you get to the bottom of why you're not super blooming in this area of your life, ready to reveal these thieves and foxes before they ruin any more of the potential in this very important area of your life.

Chapter Eight

Inspecting the Foundation

The first thing you have to do is locate these lies. But where are they? We all have them, but how do we find them? Most of the time, they will find us.

When it comes to relationships, we usually don't see them until they're staring us in the face with fangs bared. They can be like silent gas leaks deep in our hearts, and we never know about them until a little spark on the right trigger, the right turn of phrase, or the right situation, and then—*boom*.

When David and I were newlyweds, I still had a lot of these gas leaks. Being in an intimate relationship with me was like taking a stroll through the rice paddies of postwar Vietnam. There were land mines hidden everywhere just waiting to be detonated. It was common for me in the first two years of our marriage to blow up at the smallest things. I was learning to recognize the areas of deep hurt and offense in my heart that had been left behind by my childhood and first marriage. I was living on a hair trigger, in hypervigilant self-protection mode at all times. Do you remember how I overreacted when I first met David in my front yard? Well, that didn't get any better. I jumped to conclusions quickly and processed everything as aggression toward me. I was living in a constant state of fight-or-flight. Everything from my husband's tone of voice to certain words and scenarios tied to negative past experiences would set me off into a flurry of self-preservation.

It didn't make it any easier that we were a blended family. There is a reason the word "blended" rhymes with "offended," and there were more than enough opportunities for me to feel as if I were being bullied, deceived, and/or baited. My damaged heart lens was magnifying everything that happened into a level 10/10 situation. I have to be honest with you, if it weren't for the grace of God and the supernatural patience of my husband, our marriage would not have made it through those early years.

An Ounce of Prevention...

I want to help you so you don't have to spend the first few months or years of your marriage fussing and fighting with the love of your life. So many people spend *years* ignoring or medicating the mystery pain in their hearts until they wake up one day smack-dab in the middle of a divorce, affair, bankruptcy, or physical sickness. It doesn't have to be that way. God is inviting you to repair these gas leaks and defuse these ticking time bombs before they go off and destroy your future. An ounce of prevention is worth a pound of cure. Instead of ending up in couples therapy a few years after the wedding, why not save your marriage before it even starts? We wrongly assume it will only be the *big* things, such as serial cheating, financial ruin, unexpected tragedies, or drug and alcohol addictions, that can destroy our future connections. You might be telling yourself that as long as your relationship doesn't have any of those variables, everything will be fine. But the truth is, the *big* things start out as small things. Things such as poverty mindsets, offenses, resentments, filters, prejudices, assumptions, and misunderstandings. These are the things that hinder intimacy and trust, and without intimacy and trust, even the most promising and passionate connections will eventually fizzle out.

This Sounds Like Lots of Work

Whew . . . the single life might be looking really good right about now. You might be thinking, *This sounds like a lot of work.* But even if you did have the God-given grace to go through life as an unmarried woman, you would still need to do your heart work. These cracks are not just affecting your love life; they are affecting every area of your life as well as every relationship in your life.

> An ounce of prevention is worth a pound of cure. Instead of ending up in couples therapy a few years after the wedding, why not save your marriage before it even starts?

I know we think the people in Bible days were *so* spiritual, but they were just like us. They didn't want to do their heart work either. They wanted to skip right to the good stuff.

Jesus was talking to his disciples about marriage. They were feeling the same way as all of us: "Hey this sounds hard. Maybe we shouldn't even get married at all."

Jesus responds acknowledging that marriage isn't for the faint of heart.

> *"Not everyone is **mature enough** to live a married life.*
> *It requires a certain aptitude and **grace**. Marriage*
> *isn't for everyone. Some, from birth seemingly,*
> *never give marriage a thought. Others never get*
> *asked—or accepted. And some decide not to get*
> *married for kingdom reasons. But if you're **capable***
> *of growing into the largeness of marriage, do it."*
> —MATTHEW 19:11–12 MSG (EMPHASIS MINE)

Jesus is saying, "Your Father in Heaven created you for this, but not everyone wants to go through the process to get ready for it. But if you do, there is a grace and an aptitude available for you from heaven, and if you're willing to be stretched into the largeness and weightiness of a heavenly partnership, you should do it." He was basically telling them you can live small, or you can live large. It's up to you, but you were created to live large.

God Is a Good Daddy

God loves to give us good and perfect gifts, and marriage is one of those gifts. But just like any good parent, he doesn't want to give us things that we're not yet mature enough to handle…yet.

> *The blessing of the Lord–it makes [truly] rich, and He*
> *adds no sorrow with it [neither does toiling increase it].*
> —PROVERBS 10:22 AMPC

God loves you. He doesn't want to give you something that's going to cause you to fall apart at the seams; remember he knit you together and he knows what you can handle. You wouldn't give your five-year-old the keys to the family car. That would not be good parenting. I just read an article about a five-year-old in Utah who stole the family SUV while his mom was napping and headed to California to buy a Lamborghini with the three dollars he had in his wallet. He was busted by the Utah Highway Patrol just three miles into his joyride. Pretty impressive and mature (if not criminal) for a kindergartener whose feet barely reached the pedals. The typical child that age would have wrecked before even getting the car out of the driveway.

Baby Gates

As parents it's our assignment to watch our children and know what responsibilities they can handle and when they can handle them. Good parents put up boundaries to keep their children out of areas that may cause them harm. We call those boundaries "baby gates." It's not that we don't want our children to climb the stairs or go into the kitchen. We just know there are some elements of those places they're not ready to navigate yet, and when they do go to those places, we take them by the hand to help them do those things safely. As soon as they show us they are mature enough, we take the baby gates down and give them free rein. As good parents we watch our children closely and know when they are ready for *more*.

We love to see our kids grow. We will even buy them clothes that are a little too big for them because we know that they are going to grow into them. We can see their potential and know they are going to grow soon, and they are going to grow a lot.

It's pleasing to us as parents to give our children room to grow but with that growth comes more responsibility. We want them to be able to drive a car, go on a date, or get their first job. We want to put more responsibility on them, but responsibility can be weighty so first we need to make sure they can handle it. So we add just enough to mature them, but not so much that it hurts them.

Cracks in the Foundation

The second that you asked God to bring you a husband, he started inspecting your foundation to see if you could handle the upgrade. If you're a homeowner and you call a contractor because you want to add on a sunroom, or office, or extension, the first thing they will do is check your foundation. They want to see if your house can handle the added weight you want to put on it. That's why you're reading this book. God wants to add weight to your life. He wants to promote you to married, but he doesn't want to hurt you in the process.

There are some foundation repairs that need to happen so that add-on can be successful. This is why so many people run into problems in relationships. Intimacy is heavy. The reason you've been failing in love is that the lies you're believing gave your heart a crumbling foundation that can't support the weight of the romance you want.

In your past relationships, you might have tried to jump over those God-given baby gates. When one relationship fell apart, you went right out and tried another and then another. You didn't want to stay single long enough to find out *why* you keep choosing dysfunctional relationships; you just wanted to avoid the pain of loneliness, so you jumped out of the frying pan and into the fire. Rebounding is always a bad idea. I call it "trying again with no new information or maturity." It's almost always a recipe for a new failure and usually the main reason for an "it's complicated" Facebook relationship status.

> Rebounding is always a bad idea. I call it "trying again with no new information or maturity."

All this heaviness from past heartbreaks can make everything seem more complicated. You never know if what you're feeling has to do with what is happening in your current relationship or if it's left over from one of your past failed attempts at love that you've never given yourself time to process. We have a bad habit of continuing to medicate a problem instead of getting to the root of it. Often when people feel the weight of a relationship is too heavy, they do exactly the wrong thing and try to add another addition to an already crumbling foundation. That addition might be a puppy, a home, a business, or even a baby. *Never* a good idea. Imagine that you're treading water, barely able to keep your head up, and someone tosses you a baby—you're drowning for sure now.

Revealing for a Healing

Right now, think of the Holy Spirit as your contractor, here to help you inspect your foundation and make any necessary repairs. When it comes to these heart cracks, we can't just erase them—we need to replace them. We can't just cover them up, we have to fill them in with the concrete of absolute truth.

Let's revisit the idea of permission. Through this entire process it's going to be important for you to keep giving God permission to help you get to the bottom of things. Reread that permission slip as much as needed to find these lies we are believing, these false lives we have been living, and let him reveal them to us.

Reveal simply means "to make something known through divine inspiration." I like to call this process a "Revealing for a Healing." But if you have a Do Not Disturb sign or a Keep Out sign on specific memories or areas of your life, God will not trespass. He must be permitted to enter. God is a giver, and one of the most beautiful gifts he has given us is free will (or choice). He respects our boundaries, and he is not going to force anything on you. And while he will not force you to deal with anything you're not ready to deal with, he will continue to love you and ask you to invite him into these damaged areas of your heart to restore your full potential.

You may have been through some terrible things in life, and you're worried if they come out, your whole life will fall apart. You don't have to worry about that; God is a master Jenga player. If you have never played Jenga, it's the game that consists of a wooden block tower and the goal is to strategically remove one of those blocks when it's your turn; you know that if you pull out the wrong block first, the whole thing will come tumbling down. Some things must come to light first in our hearts before other things can be revealed. God knows the perfect way to heal your heart without causing any more collateral damage.

This heart work will consist of four parts:

Revealing—*First start with the most significant problem areas in your life. These troubled areas are an indication that lies are being believed in these areas and they need healing. Ask the Holy Spirit to show you the lie you are believing in these areas, and with your permission the Holy Spirit will supernaturally peel back the counterfeit layers and help you uncover and see the roots of all the lies that are keeping you stuck.*

Repentance—*Then you will verbally come out of agreement with all the lies, vows, and counterfeits being revealed by asking for forgiveness. The word "forgiveness" literally means "to have a change of mind or heart."*

Confession—*Next you will acknowledge any unworthy behavior that you have committed against yourself and others while operating under what we now know are lies and trauma-based identities. You may be asked to confess this to others as well as to God.*

Forgiveness—*Finally you will release yourself and others from all the consequences resulting from operating under these lies. This includes releasing grudges, anger, resentment, trauma bonds, and any bitterness or unforgiveness against others or yourself.*

Afterward, ask the Holy Spirit to show you the truth about these situations and yourself. Repeat these truths to yourself regularly, and embrace scriptures and other divine confirmations of them to continue to reinforce your new belief systems. If you implement these four steps for everything that surfaces in your heart while reading this book, you will receive true closure along with a renewed sense of authentic identity.

Before we start, decide right now that you are going to reject every lie that is revealed through this process and embrace God's beautiful truth. Even if those lies are things you have been believing for a long time, and even if doing so causes you discomfort or pain to let them go. I know it seems much easier to believe the things you don't like about your life are someone else's fault than to own the idea that you have actively chosen the life you're living, misery and all. But in the long run, believing that will make your life so much harder than it has to be. There are two types of pain: the temporary kind that leads to the most amazing life changes or the permanent kind that seems to last forever.

Are you ready? Let's go catch some foxes!

Chapter Nine

Restoring the
Foundation

I was at an event several years back and I saw a beautiful painting of a lion about to pounce on its prey. The lion was ferocious yet at the same time majestic; he reminded me of Aslan in *The Chronicles of Narnia*.

This painting moved me. I was going through a particularly rough place in my life at the time, and I whispered to God, "That's what I need you to do, God, devour my enemies."

To which he responded, "Okay, but first you have to step out of the way."

"What?" I said, "I'm in the way? I don't understand."

He replied, "The enemies of your abundant life are living in your heart, and if you will stop protecting them, I will remove them for you." That's when he showed me that my heart had become a sanctuary for shame, a refuge for rejection, a safe house for scarcity—you get the point.

I was allowing all of these mindsets to live in my heart; sometimes I was even defending my right to have them there. Some of them had been there for a really long time and they were ruining my life. I had to finally step aside and allow him to remove them for me. It was the best decision I ever made.

Now it's your turn. It's time to get rid of the squatters in your heart, not rent them a room in the basement but evict them for good. To do that we will have to get down to the source, the root of the lie itself.

Basic Girl Lies

As a relationship coach, I have run into *hundreds* of lies that women believe about themselves, men, marriage, and God.

Some of these lies are so strange and so far-fetched that you wonder how anyone could ever believe them in the first place. But most of what I hear is pretty basic, and it seems as if many women struggle with the same unhealthy mindsets.

Since it would be difficult to unpack every one, I have chosen seven of the most common lies women believe. As you read this list, you will probably realize you believe or have believed some version of these lies too. I'm going to show you what the process of revealing, confessing, repenting, and forgiving looks like for all the following foundational lies. Then, as the Holy Spirit begins to show you the cracks in your foundation, those sly little foxes, you can use this same process to get free of those too.

Lie#1: It's Good to Be Independent

There are things in life we need to do for ourselves, such as brush our teeth or avoid going through the Krispy Kreme drive-through when the "Hot Doughnuts *Now*" light is on (at least, not every day). There are elements of life you can't delegate to others, such as relational conflict. You can't send your mom to make up with your best friend or send your brother to put in your two weeks' notice. You have to own those things. The other thing no one can do for you is your heart work—which is what I call the process of getting down to the lies in your heart that are holding you back and replacing them with truth.

We live in a culture that celebrates independence, especially in women. Self-reliance is romanticized; women who don't need anyone else physically or emotionally are called "queens." You pride yourself on being able to bring home the bacon *and* fry it up in the pan. But the truth is that hyper-independence is a trauma response. It's a full-blown Survivor personality. Not allowing anyone to help you or even know you need help, acting like you have it all together all the time, and feeling like you need to cross every "t" and dot every "i" by yourself is a defense mechanism.

> You might love being called "responsible" (which sounds like a good thing), but in your case, it's just a fancy word for fear.

If this describes you, you probably became this way because you learned through bad experiences that depending on other people is too risky. So instead of being disappointed by other people failing to support, protect, help, and provide for you yet again, you took responsibility yourself. From your perspective, it's not smart, safe, or even possible to depend on others. Rather than be let down again, it's much easier to depend only on yourself. You might love being called "responsible" (which sounds like a good thing), but in your case, it's just a fancy word for fear. What looks on the outside like a very put-together organized, capable, and in-control woman, is just a scared little girl inside who made the decision long ago that if she wanted a good life, she was going to have to be in charge of it and get it herself.

As a single woman, you might be getting upset by this point. After all, since you're alone, who else is there to talk to the landlord, negotiate with the mechanic, or help plan your retirement? The answer is—God.

Throughout your life, you are going to have many needs and God is the source of fulfillment for every one of those needs. However, people are the resource he will use to fulfill most, if not all, of those needs.

Think of God as the head of the human resources department. When you have a need, he sends the most qualified person to meet it. This is how many people get disappointed. They go straight to the resource—people—to meet their needs instead of going straight to the source—God. Then when people either can't or won't help them, it reinforces the lie that they can't depend on anyone.

Well, it's kind of a lie. You can only be dependent on two relationships. The first is with your parents or caregivers as a child until you can meet your basic needs on your own. The other is eternal, and that is dependence on God.

The failure of your first dependent relationship is often where this lie of independence begins. Children raised by parents who are unstable, addicts, neglectful, emotionally or physically unavailable, or sick have to start adulting very quickly.

We were not made to be independent; we were made to be dependent on God and interdependent with one another, letting God use us to help each other as he wills.

Women who believe this lie often struggle the most with having fun. That might not sound like a big deal at first, but fun is part of the essence of the healthy feminine heart.

I've interviewed hundreds of men for my matchmaking program about what they notice first about a woman. It often comes down to girlhood: their smile, their laugh, their ability to enjoy life.

When you think about it, it makes sense. After all, it's about a girl meeting a boy and falling in love.

We need to get back to the girl inside you. You know, the one who's fun, carefree, and lighthearted. The one whose face doesn't have a perpetual disgusted expression like she's smelling something rotten. The one who has joy and peace and doesn't have the weight of the world on her shoulders.

It's time to let God take the weight of the world off your shoulders.

Revealing—*Rooted in fear of abandonment, childhood neglect, disappointment, and rejection.*

Confession—*I need people. I have not been created to do life on my own. God is my source and people are only a resource. If I look to God to meet my needs, I will not be disappointed anymore by people. I don't have to be self-defended because I am God-defended.*

Repentance—*I reject the lie that it's good to go it alone. I accept that I am dependent on God and that it is good to need people. God, forgive me for not asking or receiving help from you or the people around me. For not trusting people and allowing them to care for me.*

Forgiveness—*I forgive myself for believing that I have to take care of myself and that nobody can take care of me the way I can take care of me. I forgive the people, including my parents and family, who have failed or neglected to meet my needs.*

Lie #2: I Messed Up My
Chance to Be Married

Do you think God was blindsided by your mistakes? When God wrote the story of our lives, he had already factored in our bad decisions, naivete, stubbornness, brokenness, and sometimes even our downright stupidity. I know that a few of you may be familiar with Jeremiah 29:11, but I want to show you the one word most people miss.

---

*I have it all planned out—**plans** to take
care of you, not abandon you, **plans** to
give you the future you hope for.*

—Jeremiah 29:11 MSG (emphasis mine)

I noticed a long time ago that when people read or quoted this scripture, they would say the singular word "plan" instead of the plural word "plans." He's not saying, "I know the plan I have for you and if you mess it up, you don't get another shot." He's saying, "I know the *plans* I have for you to give you this bright and amazing future."

Essentially, he's saying you can't mess up my plan because if you do, I have another one. If you give God permission, he can even use all those mistakes you made as an ingredient to bless you and make his plan better than it would have been if you'd done it "right" in the first place.

You might be thinking, *Well, oh well. I had my chance, but that ship has sailed.* News flash, sister. Your ship can't sail without you because you're the captain. It's not going anywhere without you. So many women are waiting for their ship to come in, but your ship is waiting for you to set sail.

You may have dated or known someone in college, in high school, or when you were younger who, for whatever reason or another, became "the one that got away." I've heard that Adele song many times. Maybe it was because you thought there was something better. Maybe it was your fault. Maybe he was great, and you handled things badly or even cheated.

> You might be thinking, Well, oh well. I had my chance, but that ship has sailed. News flash, sister. Your ship can't sail without you because you're the captain.

But the bottom line is, no matter what happened you weren't ready, so even if he was great, he wasn't great for you.

Maybe you think you've put this off too long. Maybe you are like my client Anne, who has pursued her career for the last several decades. Now that she's finally circling around to this area of her life and feeling that tug on her heart that she wants to be married, she's afraid she's waited too long.

Well, she hasn't. God gives us the desires of our hearts. So if the desire of your heart is to be married, that desire came from God, and he isn't going to give you a desire for something you can't have.

We've talked about how God doesn't have just one plan for your life. He doesn't have just one possible perfect husband for you either. Even if you knew the "perfect" guy for you (are you *really* sure he was perfect?) and now he's married to someone else, God still has a match made in Heaven for you. Someone who will be so amazingly matched to who you are now it will knock your socks off.

And for all my sisters who are divorced like me, you need to know that God loves you. He doesn't hate divorce; he hates why people get divorced. He hates broken covenants and abuse. But it's important for you to know that he loves his daughters more than he loves any rules.

It's time to try again. First you have to make room in your heart by letting go of the lie that you ruined your only chance at happily ever after.

Revealing—*Rooted in scarcity, regret, self-bitterness, disillusionment, and fear of failure.*

Confession—*I confess that I have believed that it is in my power to mess up the plan of God. I have believed my destiny is dependent on my own ability to make all the right choices instead of depending on God's goodness.*

Repentance—*I reject the lie that I only have one chance to make all the right choices. I renounce the poverty mentality that there was only one right option for me, and I missed it and now it's too late.*

Forgiveness—*I forgive myself for believing this lie and for any unworthy behavior that might have broken relationships in my past. I forgive anyone who might have played a role in what I perceive as missed opportunities and lost time.*

Lie #3: I Don't Deserve This

You're right. You don't deserve this.

You're never going to be able to deserve, earn, or merit anything God wants to give you.

This lie is rooted in the idea that God blesses me when I'm good and punishes me when I'm bad. You think that when you do the right things, God will bless you and when you do the wrong things, he will punish you. That's the way the world works, right? Yes, it's the way the world works, but it's not the way God works.

I remember years ago, God asked me, "Do you want to live an amazing life?"

My answer was, "Duh! Of course, I want that."

His unexpected comeback was, "Then you have to learn to receive what you do not deserve."

Say what? You have to be able to receive what you cannot earn, merit, or achieve for yourself and simply receive it from the finished work of the cross. This revelation really rocked my world because I realized that I had bought into the idea that anything and everything I wanted had to come from my own sweat equity. I had to make it happen. I had to deserve it, I had to earn it.

It makes sense that I would adopt this self-sufficient attitude coming from my background of being a troubled child and teen, living in a girls home and foster care-type situations. It is easy to fall into an orphan mindset when you're, well, an orphan.

I wasn't good at receiving at all, which is the *opposite* of the healthy feminine you and I have been created to be. I was constantly striving and believing that I had to be perfect in every area. Whether it was love, gifts from other people, or even just help with doing simple things, I felt the need to earn anything that was given to me.

How good are you at receiving? Do you allow people to help you? Can you let your friend pick up the check at lunch? When people ask, "How can I help you?" do you have a ready list of areas where you can receive their generous offer of assistance? Here's an easy one—when someone offers you a compliment about your hair, your new dress, or your pretty smile, do you respond with gratitude or with dismissal? Perhaps you'll even outright argue with them about how the compliment is completely undeserved.

How good are you at receiving from God?

Do you sit yourself down in the waiting room when you haven't performed perfectly? Do you tell yourself that God can't bless you with the desires of your heart until you reach a future state of perfection? A state that you're never able to reach, so time and time again you find yourself in a stagnant cycle just waiting to be good enough to be blessed?

Perfectionism is fear. It's fear of rejection, of not being enough. (Spoiler alert: you're not perfect and you don't have to be for God, but with God you're more than enough.) In case you haven't caught on yet, this is not a 50/50 relationship. You take one step toward God, and he comes running the rest of the way to you. He's not expecting you to be perfect because Jesus already took care of that. So stop worrying that you're going to screw up and let God down.

You can't let God down because you're not holding him up.

Revealing—*Rooted in perfectionism, unforgiveness, fear of rejection, spirit of religion, pride.*

Confession—*I confess I have tried to earn the love of God and people by doing everything right. I have rejected the goodness of God and people because of my need to earn or merit everything that is given to me.*

Repentance—*I come out of agreement with perfectionism, fear of rejection, and pride. I ask for forgiveness from striving and trying to earn the love of God and others through my performance.*

Forgiveness—*I forgive myself for being so hard and critical toward myself and others and for trying to earn what Jesus did for me on the cross. I forgive myself for not allowing myself to be loved just as I am and enjoying the completely undeserved blessings of God.*

Lie #4: There Are No Good Men

I meet so many women who tell me that there are just no good men left on the earth. All the good ones are already taken. Let's all just take a moment to laugh at that. There are 7.67 billion people in the world—and you just need *one*. I promise that there are good, healthy, emotionally and spiritually mature men among them *and there's one for you.*

You might be thinking, *Well, Jackie, that's a bit hypocritical. How can you be so sure there are good men when you have a whole chapter of this book talking about how bad they are?*

I wasn't talking about how bad they are. I was talking about how we have all been changed by pain and not for the better. Just like you made the decision to break free from all your shame and fear-based identities, along with all the behavior patterns that are unworthy of a daughter of God, there are men who have done the same. Lots of them.

We don't have a "no good man" problem; we have a judgment problem.

If I had to describe a man to someone who had never seen one before based on the things women tell me they believe about men, the description would read as follows:

Men are dishonest, aggressive, unfeeling, unfaithful, unreliable, carnal, weak, passive, manipulative, violent, lazy, selfish, controlling, abusive, narcissistic, immature, ungodly, uncaring, power hungry, deadbeat con artists who only want one thing—sex.

Oh, and let's not forget that they're also intimidated by successful, smart, beautiful women.

C'mon... give me a break. That sounds pretty pathetic. All the men I know love smart, beautiful, and successful women. If you don't know one good man, you have to question your perceptions or your chosen community, but either way the buck has to stop with you. We have to take responsibility for the things we have chosen to believe.

The truth is that as the pendulum has swung over the last seventy years to empower women (which is amazing), it has simultaneously disempowered men. We want strong men, but we don't want them to be *too* strong because we never want history to repeat itself again. Where are all the good men?

> It's not that there aren't good men. It's that we don't always like good men.

My husband, David, and I have begun working with men as part of our matchmaking program, and I can confirm that the good men are in the same place you are. They're working their jobs, going about their hobbies, hanging out with friends and family on the weekends, doing volunteer work, and most of them are wondering where all the good women are. If you think men don't want to be married, I assure you that there are many, many who do and are just as frustrated as you in their inability to find their person.

But let's be honest. It's not that there aren't good men. It's that we don't always *like* good men. Some of you really like the bad boys. They are your "type," and the good guys don't have any chance whatsoever with you. You say there are no good guys, but when you're presented with a good guy, you're like "Next!"

For a long time, men have been the scapegoat for everything wrong with the world, but the blame game keeps men and women in opposition, pointing fingers and helping no one.

So often I hear this phrase: "A man needs to pursue me." Does he? Really? Are you running away? That phrase gets thrown around mostly in church circles, but it is not anywhere in the Bible regarding romance or marriage. I checked. We absolutely need reciprocation. A relationship can't sail when only one person is rowing, but the idea that the man needs to walk straight up to you, ask for your number, and keep asking until you cave in is unhealthy and kind of creepy.

> Healthy men are not interested in climbing walls. Do you know who climbs walls? Thieves climb walls; worthy suitors knock at the front door.

But let's face it; that's exactly what a lot of us have gone for in the past. That's what rom-coms and a generation of soap operas have taught us love should look like, right? Wrong.

Healthy men are not interested in climbing walls. Do you know who climbs walls? Thieves climb walls; worthy suitors knock at the front door. They want to come into your living room, not your bedroom. They respect your power of choice, and if you say "no," they will respect that too.

Believe there are good guys in the world. Learn to look for good guys. Learn to say "yes" to the good guys. They are there, I promise.

> **Revealing**—*Rooted in bitterness, hatred, unforgiveness, judgment, scarcity, and pride.*
> **Confession**—*I confess that I have been sexist. I have believed that men are all bad and that my singleness is their fault. I have judged all men by what a few have done, and I have not seen them as the incredible, gifted, talented, and precious sons of God that they are.*
> **Repentance**—*I come out of agreement with the lie that there are no good men. I ask God to help me see men as they are and not through the filters of my flawed beliefs that come from my past experiences.*
> **Forgiveness**—*I ask for forgiveness for judging all men based on a few. I forgive the men in my past and in my life who have hurt, misused, and mistreated me. I forgive myself for choosing unhealthy men out of a scarcity mindset and my own lack of self-worth.*

Lie #5: If It's God Working, It Will Be Easy/Convenient

Far too often, we cut and run at the first sign of opposition. We think that if something is "from God," then it won't challenge us, stretch us, or refine us. That's simply not true.

All of life is about growth, and growth means transforming and changing. This doesn't mean that God is going to destroy everything you currently love about your life for the sake of the "greater good." But it does mean we have to be willing to let go of the lesser thing if we want to have more.

For instance, you might meet an amazing guy who could be straight from your dreams, but he has kids. Maybe he lives a town over, a time zone over, or even on another continent. It could be he's from a different ethnicity, cultural background, and/or race and you're worried what your family will think or that you won't like the food at his family Thanksgiving dinners. Maybe he's in the military, law enforcement, or some other job that makes him work odd hours and doesn't let him move. Perhaps he's not from the same religious background as you, or he's much older or younger than you imagined he would be.

Some of you don't even want to date. You swear you won't date. You want to just *know* when you meet the one. You want the clouds to part and a light to shine down and a voice to come from Heaven that says, "This is your husband in whom I am well pleased."

You have no intention of leaving your zip code, your comfort zone, your house, or even your couch. If God is going to give you a man, he better deliver him straight to your door.

You don't even want him shipped via USPS; you want him shipped via Amazon Prime. You know . . . with the tracking information updated every ten minutes and a notification on your phone once he's dropped off. *Ding!* "Your husband is at the front door. Tell us how we did!"

If you're demanding that God do this without any action on your part, then I am here to tell you that you need to let go of that mindset right now. I can't promise what this process will look like, but I can promise that it will stretch you.

Isra is a young woman from our worship community here in the U.S. She had been believing God for a husband for years without any promising prospects. She visited Canada on a trip to visit friends right before the COVID-19 lockdowns and met an amazing guy there at a home gathering.

> Sometimes you're not stretched by geography, you're just stretched by biography. Either way, there will be *something* that challenges you.

They began dating long-distance during the COVID-19 lockdowns but with international restrictions, Isra and her guy were only able to see each other a handful of times over their eleven months of dating. In February 2021, while record-breaking ice storms blew in from the south, Isra hopped in her little car and made the twenty-plus-hour journey through ice, sleet, and snow to the Canadian border.

Once she was there, Isra had to undergo a fourteen-day quarantine at a hotel, still not able to see her guy. (Because of COVID, remember?)

Isra spent those fourteen days in lockdown, by herself. I have no idea how she didn't claw the walls down in boredom during that time because I certainly would have, but she got out and was finally able to see her boyfriend.

Well, guess what? He proposed (after all that, he better, right?) and she said yes! As I write this, they recently got married (and she has moved to Canada).

Sometimes you walk out in your front yard and meet the man of your dreams, like I did. The geography didn't stretch me but blending families and working through our pasts did. Sometimes you relocate to the other side of the world. Sometimes you're not stretched by geography, you're just stretched by biography. Either way, there will be *something* that challenges you.

You might want to avoid the tough stuff. You might want to do everything your own way, but how's your way working out for you? It's time to do things God's way. Trust me; it's always a much better choice.

Revealing—*Rooted in control, fear of change, unforgiveness, bitterness, pride, and unbelief.*
Confession—*I confess that I have not been willing to do my part but have expected God to do his part. I have resisted change. I have resisted being challenged or stretched in order to receive the desire of my heart.*
Repentance—*I come out of agreement with the idea that if it's supernatural, it will be simple, and it will take no effort or sacrifice on my part. I repent for embracing doubt because I've taken risks and things haven't worked out in the past.*

Forgiveness—*I forgive myself for being apathetic, for insisting that I need to be in control. I forgive others for not reciprocating sacrifices I have made for them. I ask for forgiveness for not trusting God that change will be for my good and for clinging to my own way instead of to his way.*

Lie #6: I'm Damaged Goods

I'm not dismissing your pain. Some of the things that have happened to you are terrible. I've been accused in the past of minimizing abuse because I don't allow a lot of feeling sorry for ourselves in my coaching. But I want you to know that I'm not minimizing abuse—I am maximizing the cross.

I'm an adult survivor of sexual, mental, and verbal abuse and of neglect and abandonment. But abuse is not my story, and it's not your story. "Abuse" is a word that's used to describe the weapon that the enemy used to try to keep us out of the destiny God has designed for us. I refuse to allow it to take center stage in my life as a main character. The enemy's plot and plan didn't succeed with me, and I don't want them to succeed with you either.

God told me many years ago that I could have my "story"—the one about abuse, betrayal, abandonment, hurt, and pain—or I could have his story about my life start with the story of Jesus dying for me on the cross. But I couldn't have both.

I chose the one with Jesus.

I recently saw a post on social media that said, "We have all been so hurt by somebody that it changed us forever." How about changing our confession to, "We've all been so loved by somebody that it changed us forever"?

Nothing anybody has ever done to us is greater than what Jesus did for us on the cross. You need to know that regardless of what society might be saying, you don't have to take on a posture of victimhood to receive justice from God. There are no trophies for trauma. If pain becomes your claim to fame, then you cannot be delivered from that cycle because you have chosen pain to be your identity.

People who are stuck in a Victim identity say things such as: "They ruined my life," "I can't recover," "I can't get over this," "This will never be fixed," "It's not fair," or "I'm damaged goods."

It's time to take your identity back.

Nothing has more power over your destiny than what you assign to it. Forgiveness assigns the power over our destiny back to God, not to the people and things that have hurt us. Forgiveness says, "Yes, this hurt me, but it's not going to kill me because my identity is much bigger than what has happened to me. Nothing I've gone through in this life can change who God says I am and the good plans he has for my life."

Many of the things that have happened in your life were not part of God's original plan for you. The one thing I want you to remember is if it wasn't good, it didn't come from God, but if you give it to him now, he certainly can turn it around and use it to bless you.

You intended to harm me, but God intended
it for good to accomplish what is now
being done, the saving of many lives.

—Genesis 50:20 NIV

Your life has value. It has the ability to change someone's life. People need someone who has been there to help reframe the hurt and confusion they are feeling and open their eyes to the joy of transformation. Just like I'm doing for you right now through this book.

When you choose God's ending to your story, he will use your story to change the world.

Revealing—*Self-hatred, bitterness, unforgiveness, self-pity, unworthiness, shame.*
Confession—*I have believed that the tragedies in my past have ruined my future. I have believed that what has happened to me, what has been done to me, and the dark chapters in my life were stronger than God and his goodness.*
Repentance—*I repent for doubting God's power to restore and redeem me. I come out of agreement with the lie that the redemption of Jesus is not enough for me. I receive and I surrender to his healing grace in my life and the beautiful purpose he has for my pain.*

> **Forgiveness**—*I forgive those who have hurt me in the past. I bless and release them to God. I forgive myself for any poor choices or bad decisions that caused me to be hurt, and I release myself from shame, guilt, and blame.*

Lie #7: God Doesn't Want This for Me

God wants you to be married more than you want to be married. Surprised?

I recently heard something profound: "A lot of times we like to create theology to explain away our pain." I have seen this happen time and time again as well-meaning pastors and women's ministry leaders spout out one-liners such as, "God must just have a different assignment for you in this season" or, "I think God just wants you to focus on serving him right now."

You know the type—bottle-blonde with platinum highlights, manicured nails to show off her three-carat wedding ring, wears cardigans and ankle boots even in summer, and posts selfies of herself and her husband (who looks like freaking Ryan Gosling) with hashtags like #SoBlessed. Kind of makes you want to hit someone, doesn't it? "Easy for you to say, picture-perfect married lady. Can't you see I'm dying of loneliness here?"

While I'm sure these teachers have good intentions, I think we both know these ideas aren't helping. At best, you let them talk you into the waiting room ("It's just not God's timing"). You might even let them convince you that you have some assignment or task to complete before God will let you move into the next season of your life ("God must want you to focus on volunteering and serving others right now").

Hopefully by now you know that you aren't supposed to be waiting and that you can't earn this. God isn't up there with some kind of celestial punch card, counting off the number of mission trips you've been on or the number of homeless people you've fed until you finally get enough stars to earn a husband.

"But Jackie," you might be saying, "what about the gift of singleness Paul talked about?" Yeah, let's talk about that.

In 1 Corinthians 7, Paul talks about how it's better to be single than married and how he wishes everyone had the gift of singleness. The first thing we almost always miss when reading this passage is that Paul is giving his opinion. While Paul was a great leader of the faith, and I think we can all agree he had some important opinions, he says multiple times throughout this chapter that it's Paul speaking, not God.

The second and most important thing to know is that the word "gift" there is *charisma*. It's the same word used for supernatural endowments of the Holy Spirit, like healings or miracles. What Paul is talking about is a paranormal phenomenon that allows some people not to want the companionship and intimacy of an earthly romantic partner.

We can't just read the Bible; we have to *read* the Bible. Why might Paul say he wishes everyone had the gift of singleness like him? After all, if everyone had the gift, the human species wouldn't last long. He was watching people suffer and some people suffer even more because of their attachments to their wives, husbands, and children. Paul is addressing an audience of Christians who are under persecution and facing martyrdom daily. So Paul is saying that it's easier to lay your life down when you aren't worried about what's going to happen to your family and you can fully focus on the work of the King because you're not entangled with domestic affairs.

You're here because you want to be here, and you want to be here because God wants you to be here.

One sure way to know you don't have the gift of singleness is that you crave romantic intimacy. If you have a sex drive, you don't have the gift of singleness. I have met people who genuinely have the supernatural endowment, that *charisma*, to be single, and I promise you that they don't want spouses, they don't want children, and they don't listen to Celine Dion songs on repeat while crying into a pint of ice cream over their last failed relationship.

You're here because you want to be here, and you want to be here because God wants you to be here.

Psalm 37:4 tells us that the desires of our hearts—those persistent longings that no number of bad dates, bad experiences, or bad break-ups can stop—come from God. If you're reading this book, you want to be married. If you're reading this book, God wants you married.

"What if this is just my desire?" you might be saying. "What if this didn't come from God?"

Stop. Just stop. Your desires are given to you to direct you toward your destiny. Our broken hearts have desires, true. Our broken desires can have us pick the wrong guys or turn down the right ones, but the desire for marriage comes from God.

If you want marriage, you were made for marriage. God has a love story just for you. God is on your side in this. Get excited about that!

Revealing—*Fear, unbelief, rejection, bitterness toward God and self, scarcity, unforgiveness.*

Confession—*I confess I have believed God was holding out on me, that he didn't intend to give me the desires of my heart. That I am forsaken, forgotten, and not important to him or his plan. That he is not emotionally involved with my life or my future. I confess that I am not happy for others when they get the things that I want and have not gotten ... yet.*

Repentance—*I reject the lie that God doesn't want a good marriage for me. I repent of believing that God doesn't have a husband for me and for blaming God for my singleness and failed relationships. I ask God for help seeing him as the good father he wants to be to me.*

Forgiveness—*I forgive myself for believing that God doesn't have good things for me, but he has them for everyone else. I ask to be forgiven for jealousy and accusing God and others of withholding good things from me. I forgive God for not letting me have the things my broken heart thought I wanted, and I ask for help in gaining his perspective in this area.*

Chapter Ten

Reclaiming the Feminine Heart

Y ou should already be beginning to feel some healing and clarity coming to your heart. As we continue to allow God to get down to the deep root systems, the freer we will become and with that freedom will come more changed behavior.

You know the behaviors that are causing you trouble? Like maxing out your credit cards, eating an extra row of Oreos, dating a guy you "knew was trouble when he walked in," having sex outside of a covenant relationship, screaming at the cashier when they take an extra ten seconds to bag your groceries, drinking a whole bottle of wine by yourself . . . every night. You want to change these things. You don't like these things, but try as you might, you can never change them. At least not for long.

You may have asked yourself, *Why do I keep seeing this movie? I don't like this movie. So why do I keep buying a ticket? Why do I keep going on this same merry-go-round and never make any progress?* Why is that? It's because so much of what we do is unconscious. If you want to think of it this way, you're on counterfeit-identity-autopilot most of the time.

And all that other crazy stuff you do? Identity is what's driving it.

No Fake It 'Til You Make It

You probably think that your identity is whatever you declare it to be. I know you like cute positive affirmations. Maybe you've got a list taped to your bathroom mirror that you run through every morning. I love declarations and confessions too. I do them every day. They're awesome. They're great. Don't stop.

The problem is that you might *know* those things and want to believe them in your mind, but the *truth* of those things has never made it down that eighteen-inch journey to your heart. They can't get in there because that space is littered with all kinds of drama, trauma, lies, and offense. So you're saying those things, but you're not living those things because life is a heart game, not a head game.

> The problem is that you might *know* those things and want to believe them in your mind, but the *truth* of those things has never made it down that eighteen-inch journey to your heart.

So whatever we *really* believe about ourselves—not in our heads, but our hearts—our behaviors will follow that.

I want to talk to you about the law of attraction. When I first started talking about the biblical law of attraction, I got a lot of hate. Oh, my goodness. Honey, people went crazy. They were like "What's this New Age *crap*?!"

Well, it's not New Age, it's the Bible. The Bible doesn't say "law of attraction," but the concept is there. It's not my fault if the psychics, mystics, and spiritual gurus are using this principle better than the Christians. Our God invented it; we should be putting it to work for ourselves.

What You Believe, You Become;
What You Become, You Attract

The lies you're discovering right now as you go through the process in the previous chapters matured over time and have been reinforced over time. As I've already told you, the more you believe the lie, the more you speak the lie. So if I believe the lie that men can't be trusted, I'll say to my happily engaged friend, "Men can't be trusted. Better get a prenup while you can!"

I know a beautiful young woman who is a successful small business owner. She is also engaged to be married. On more than one occasion, this young woman has instructed me to make sure I am protecting my financial interests for the day that my husband "inevitably" cheats on me and leaves me for someone else.

I said, "Wait, aren't you engaged to be married to an amazing man?"

She said, "Oh yes. I love my fiancé. He's wonderful. But this is just what men do. We women have to protect ourselves and cover all our bases, so that when they find something better and leave us, we women won't be left holding the bag."

Why is she saying that? Because some trauma in her life has told her that's true and now that lie has grown. It's multiplied and taken up so much space in her heart that it's overflowing out of her mouth. God tells us it's out of the abundance of our heart that our mouth communicates.

*A good man brings good things out of the good
stored up in his heart, and an evil man brings evil
things out of the evil stored up in his heart. For
the mouth speaks what the heart is full of.*

—LUKE 6:45 NIV (EMPHASIS MINE)

If you ever want to find out what you believe, what
you *really* believe, just listen to yourself talking to others
sometime. Not when you have planned the "right" thing
to say, not when you're making those declarations of
what you want to be true—just your everyday conversations. If you pay attention,
you will see a pattern—and it
might not be a good one. You
may not realize it's a big deal.
They're just words, right? But
they don't just stay words.
Your weekly rant about what
you hate (insert topic) isn't
harmless at all. It has power.

> Whatever we're
> communicating,
> we will eventually
> manifest in some
> form or fashion.

Do you believe words
have power? If you don't,
why are you making those
declarations? Why do you care when you are criticized
or when people speak negative things about you? You
clearly believe on some level that what is said affects
what happens in your life. The reason you believe that is
that it's true.

Whatever we're communicating, we will eventually manifest in some form or fashion. We start attracting what we're talking about. If I'm like this young woman, I start attracting men who don't take care of me. Men who will abandon me and won't provide. Because that's my only experience, I continue to believe it. I'm not attracting the good guys. I'm only attracting what I believe to be true about guys, so I believe more and more that all guys are that way. It becomes a self-perpetuating and self-fulfilling prophecy.

Biblical Law of Attraction

"But Jackie," you might be saying, "that just says that what's in our hearts comes out of our mouths. There's nothing in that verse about those things being drawn back to us."

Hold on; I'm getting there:

From the fruit of their mouth a person's stomach is filled; with the harvest of their lips they are satisfied. The tongue has the power of life and death, and those who love it will eat its fruit.

—Proverbs 18:20-21 NIV

Luke 6:45 teaches us that what's in our heart, we speak, and Proverbs 18:20-21 teaches us that what we speak, we create. We're all going to eat our words, more or less.

So while this young woman who believes all men are unfaithful isn't attracting the good guys, it's not because there are no good guys.

Remember how I told you when you're in Victim mode, you're driving in that beat-up car? Well, you're going to attract all the people with their beat-up cars too. Whatever is in our hearts, that's what we're going to project into the world. Whatever image we are projecting, we attract back: like attracts like, counterfeit attracts counterfeit, unhealthy attracts unhealthy. Victim attracts the victimizer.

I once had an opportunity to meet a renowned missionary. This man was known for going to some of the most dangerous parts of the world to preach the gospel to people in countries that are under some of the harshest anti-Christian regimes on the globe. The kind of countries where soldiers carry really big, really scary guns at airports and where people are still publicly whipped and stoned—legally.

As a person who's passionate about justice and as a feminist, I feel the plight of these women strongly. After talking to this missionary about wanting to help set the women of those countries free, he warned me never to go to these countries.

> Whatever image we are projecting, we attract back: like attracts like, counterfeit attracts counterfeit, unhealthy attracts unhealthy. Victim attracts the victimizer.

"Well, I wasn't planning on it," I said. "But why?"

He said, "Because the men will feel the hate you have for them in your heart, and they will kill you."

I didn't know that I was projecting hate for those men. I thought I just loved the women, my sisters in those nations. I didn't realize I hated those men for the father who abandoned me, the boyfriends who cheated on me, the boys who spread rumors about me at school, the men who tried to gang rape me in the back of a car before I divinely escaped, and the former husband who emotionally abandoned and alienated me.

Even though I didn't know it, this missionary could see it in me.

It's the same way with everything and everyone. People can feel if you have hatred or anger toward them, yourself, or someone else. When you are operating within that hatred and that anger, good men will steer clear, but the kinds of men who caused your past wounds will be drawn to you.

You know the last guy you picked? The one who seemed healthier than all the others? He had a cool shirt on and a different pickup line and you thought, *This guy is different!*

Well, guess what? There was a healthy guy standing right next to him, but you didn't see that guy. You only saw the guy who ended up hurting you because he was what your belief systems were attracting, though you probably didn't know it at the time.

It's very important that we take responsibility for these blind spots and filters because until we admit the ball is in our court, we will be stuck playing the same losing game over and over.

Guilty until Proven Innocent

If you're in Survivor mode you will pride yourself that you never get the wool pulled over your eyes. You're the one who doesn't let the lyin', cheatin', cold, dead beatin', two timin', double dealin', mean, mistreatin', lovin' hearts within a mile radius. You "know" them at a first glance, and you chase them off with a ten-foot pole.

I remember one woman said to me, "I can spot a fake a mile away."

I asked her, "Can you spot a sincere guy a mile away? No, you can't. Because you're looking for a fake, and what you're looking for, you will find." Remember what I said about setting my search filter to show me only red dresses? This is a perfect example of that Survivor personality in full effect. When we scrutinize others under the magnifying glass of our fear of getting hurt, we will eventually find something to use as an excuse to disengage.

> When we scrutinize others under the magnifying glass of our fear of getting hurt, we will eventually find something to use as an excuse to disengage.

That thing we find may be real or it may just be a figment of our warped-by-trauma imaginations. We women have become so good at looking for the bad in guys that sometimes we will see it when it isn't even there. (Remember how I assumed David was a sex offender the first time I met him?) Victims will run past all the warning and "Keep Out" signs. Survivors will scream "Hell, naw!" and hit the brakes at the first sign there's a pebble in the road. Both ways will prevent you from receiving the love you deserve.

We Can't Go on Together with Suspicious Minds

As women we often put far too much stock in our intuition. When you have a wounded heart, intuition will turn into suspicion very quickly. Not every "trigger" in a budding relationship is a danger sign. When you have a negative reaction to something somebody else does, you have to ask yourself why? Is it an unhealed part of yourself that you need to dissect? Or is it your spirit telling you *No*? To learn to discern the difference, you have to pay attention to the emotions the "trigger" brings with it.

Any form of fear or anxiety is pointing to an unhealed part of your heart, and God does not lead us by fear. He will not use a panic attack to keep you out of a bad relationship. He doesn't give you a nightmare about your last date to make sure you don't go on a second date.

Regardless of whether that guy is for you, these types of reactions to trying to get to know someone else are born out of fear.

I have had many clients who will talk themselves out of getting to know someone because of a minor issue. They turn molehills into mountains because of their own fear of making another mistake. Basically, they are living their lives from a trauma response.

Everything is bad until it's proven good, and everyone is untrustworthy until they're proven trustworthy.

I had a client in my dating mentorship who posted about a first date she had gone on with a guy. They'd met on a dating app, the meet-up had gone well, and she'd had fun. A few hours later, the guy accidentally texted her a message meant for someone else that indicated he also wanted to get to know another woman in a different city. (He used those exact words, by the way: "Get to know.") My client shared a screenshot of the message in our private mentorship group asking me and her peers for advice.

Now, anyone who has used these apps knows it's not practical to talk only to one person at a time if you want to make any progress. The number of people you have to tell "Hi, how are you?" before you get to a phone call, much less an actual in-person meeting, kind of guarantees you have to be chatting up at least two or three if you want a date anytime in the near future.

I didn't see anything surprising or suspicious in the message, but her post was quickly flooded with comments from well-meaning sisters convinced that this man was trying to take advantage of her, that he was a player. One woman accused him of being sent out to groom women for sex trafficking.

Say what? The guy sent her the wrong message. I've sent messages to the wrong person too. All he said was that there was another girl in another city he wanted to get to know too. This was a low-level situation, but in just a few minutes, the heart wounds of these women took it and escalated it to DEFCON 1.

Suspicion Is Not a Gift of the Spirit

If you're like some of my clients, you will blame God or a supposed spiritual "gift" for your judgmental attitude with men. "It's not suspicion; it's my gift of intuition. It's wisdom." Is it? Really? It is true that the feminine is highly intuitive, but when our hearts are broken, those gifts are broken too. Gifts that have been overextended by trauma become a liability. Instead of being a strength, they become filters, blind spots, and a weakness.

> Gifts that have been overextended by trauma become a liability. Instead of being a strength, they become filters, blind spots, and a weakness.

Let's test this "gift" you claim is from God. Does your intuition ever tell you anything good about people? Does it ever tell you how to encourage, lift up, or speak words of affirmation over people? If not, it's not from the Spirit of love.

I had one client who was talking to a guy over an app and wasn't feeling a connection. So with no other information or incriminating evidence, she decided he must be addicted to porn and her spiritual gifts were what was turning him off. I mean . . . *wow*. That escalated quickly, don't you think?

This isn't to say that some people aren't genuinely dangerous. There are unsafe people out there, and I do advise you to use common sense safety practices when you're out and about, especially around this area of your life. For example, tell people where you are going, meet at neutral ground in public places in the beginning, and so on. You're a grown woman; you know the drill.

However, if your "gift" of intuition *only* ever says "RUN!" then it's not a gift; it's fear and self-protection masquerading as a gift and it's holding you back.

You Get What You Look for, So Look for the Good

You know that Bible verse we always quote at weddings? The one about how "Love is patient, love is kind" and so forth? The Amplified translation of that passage says, "Love is always looking for the best."

Sure, I've said several times that you need to exercise wisdom. But we need to give people the courtesy of starting out with a blank slate. When we are suspicious, we meet people for the first time and they already have all kinds of warnings, accusations, and labels scribbled on their slate.

No matter what we call it—wisdom, experience, intuition, discernment, knowing—if it's trustworthy, it should also show us good things about people and about men, even if that person remains a hard pass in the dating department. Are you able to acknowledge the gifts of your male coworker? Even if he'd be a definite "no" from you? Can you appreciate the politeness of the young man who bags your groceries every Saturday? Do you see your cousin's art talents? Are you able to see random *good* things in men?

If so, great. Keep it up. If not, you need to practice.

Learn to look for the good in people, especially in men. Learn to give people a chance to put their best foot forward. Look for the good and you attract good.

Love believes the best and you're here because you want to find love. Let's practice believing the best about one another. When we are spending our time always trying to discern if people are good or bad, we don't have any time left to love them.

God-Defended vs. Self-Defended

"But, Jackie," you might be saying, "it's a jungle out there! How can I believe the best in people when the world is out there just waiting to take advantage of me?"

This is what I call being self-defended. It's a form of that Survivor mentality we talked about. It says that you have to look out for you because no one else will, but that's not true. God is looking out for you. Will you let him?

I know it's a jungle. Remember, I'm the girl who said I came out of my mother's womb already running for my life. Everywhere I looked I saw danger, and I was always waiting for the other shoe to drop. I spent my entire life in fear to the point that I had full-blown panic disorder by the time I was twenty-one. I was afraid of everything. If something bad was going to happen to someone, I felt as if my name were at the top of that list. In my mind, the only thing that was standing between me and total destruction every day was my ability to protect myself. But even as good as I became at keeping myself alive, my ability to keep myself out of trouble was limited. I couldn't see or predict every danger before it overtook me, and I found myself in bad circumstances time and time again.

One of those times was as I was lying awake in the night trying to figure out how to fix a really bad situation. In the middle of this dark night of the soul, God asked me a question: "Who do you belong to, Jackie?" I answered immediately, "I belong to you." "Who do your problems belong to?" he continued. This time I hesitated. I wasn't sure of the correct answer. I mean, after all, this problem had been created by my own poor choices, and I was sure God expected me to fix it. Before I could answer he continued: "If you belong to me, then everything that concerns you belongs to me, including your problems." I exhaled and the tears began to flow, but he wasn't finished: "And you know what else, Jackie? I don't have any problems." Whew, God. Mic drop! That night God told me, "You've done a good job taking care of yourself so far, but I'm gonna take it from here." That night was a new beginning for me. After thirty-nine years of running for my life, I ran right into the arms of God and finally allowed him to take care of me.

You don't have to look for the dirt in people anymore. You're bound to miss some anyway, and then what? You can look for the best in people and trust that God will show you what you need to see when and if you need to see it. Justice and protection are God's department. Unlike you, he knows the true nature of someone's intention and their heart.

GOD judges persons differently than humans do. Men and women look at the face; GOD looks into the heart.

—1 SAMUEL 16:7 MSG

Divine Rejection Is Protection

Sometimes God's protection looks like not getting the "dream job" at a company that goes bankrupt six months later. Maybe your car doesn't start one morning, but you find out there was a massive pile-up on your commute route that you would have just barely missed. Like we talked about with codependency vs. interdependency, God will use the people around you to protect you.

Amy had a long history of attracting codependent, unhealthy relationships. She's a licensed therapist, and her nurturing counselor gift has gotten her into trouble when she's picked "projects" in the past. She joined my mentorship program and started dating a guy who seemed great in the beginning.

They had much in common. There were many serendipitous things about their meeting and what it took for their paths cross. It really looked like a divine connection.

A couple weeks in, Amy told me that they had broken up because of some troubling behaviors on the guy's part.

She felt bad about it and wasn't sure she'd done the right thing, but she had ended things anyway.

Amy can be picky with her taste in guys, so a few days later I started thinking that I should reach out to the guy to see if he might be interested in joining my matchmaking program. I ran it by Amy, and she was supportive, giving me his contact info.

No sooner had I texted this guy, offering him a spot in my program, than all hell broke loose. This man started accusing me and Amy of some of the most outlandish and bizarre things I'd heard in a while. He was angry, triggered, and texting in massive blocks with all caps. I was pretty surprised, to be honest.

It became clear that Amy had made a good choice in ending things; in fact, she definitely should have. This man was clearly operating in unworthy and unsafe behavior and was not in a heart space to be in a romantic relationship. I shared with Amy that things had gone badly, and we moved on.

A few weeks after my exchange with this man, Amy crossed paths with him again. Before he had blown up at me, she had been thinking about giving him another chance. Because of that incident, Amy let the guy walk right on by and didn't reconnect with him ever again.

This is an example of what it means to be God-defended. I was wrong about Amy being too picky with this guy (oh boy, was I wrong), but God used me to show Amy that this guy, at least in his current unhealed state, was bad news.

When we surrender to God and let him protect us, he does. And just like your husband will be an extension of

God's love and protection for you, your community is an extension of God's love and protection over you as well.

Man—God's Protection Plan for Women

Men were made to embody the defender nature of God. Many scientists agree that men are physically built to be fighters. They naturally have denser bones and are usually bigger and heavier. One study found that men, on average, have 75 percent more upper-body muscle and 90 percent greater upper-body strength than women. Their center of gravity is also in their upper body, which is best for when they want to punch one another. Which they seem to do a lot.

A truly masculine man is a protector. Have you ever wondered why men love video games such as *Halo* and *Call of Duty*? Their brains are getting hits of reward hormones in a way that women's brains don't. It's their "defend the home turf" programming at play.

God made men to be protectors and that includes protectors of us, not because we are weak, but because we are strong in different ways. Some women no longer take their husband's name as their own after marriage. I get it, the whole feminist ideology and not wanting to become the property of a man. But I don't see it that way because I understand the power of identity. I was overjoyed to take my husband's name and step into our new lineage and legacy together. We also take our husband's name when we get married as a symbol of covering, showing that our battles are now his battles. If someone or something wants to get at you, they will have to come through your husband to do it. In Ephesians 5, we learn that God wants husbands to protect their wives to the death just as Christ gave his life for us all. A healed, healthy, and whole masculine heart will gladly protect and, if need be, sacrifice himself for his family.

Jesus Cares Board

I want to give you a practical tip before we go any further. I know you have come this far, and I don't want to go back now. So let's keep going forward. To do that we need to put things in God's hands in a greater way than ever before. I will be the first to admit that it is easier to put things in God's hands than it is to leave things in God's hands. I'm married to a great guy and sometimes it can be tough to leave things in his hands as well.

The Bible says in 1 Peter 5:7 to cast your cares on God because he cares for you. That sounds so easy, but it can be so hard to do. I don't know about you, but I have a Jesus-take-the-wheel, no-give-it-back, no-take-it problem. That's why I have a "Jesus cares" board.

> I don't know about you, but I have a Jesus-take-the-wheel, no-give-it-back, no-take-it problem. That's why I have a "Jesus cares" board.

My Jesus cares board is just a poster board in my bedroom with 1 Peter 5:7 written at the top. It's simple, nothing fancy. Every time there is something in my life that is a situation I can't control—crazy neighbors, financial trouble, family drama—I write it down on a sticky note, stick it to the board, and say, "Okay, God. This is your problem now."

The board serves as a physical reminder that I belong to God, so my problems are his problems, and he has no problems. I pray over that board weekly and invite God into those situations. I ask him to give me strength and direction on how to do my part, but I also pray for grace to take my hands off and allow him to do his. You would be amazed by the peace that comes from taking your hands off things you cannot change or control. Let God defend you. He can do a much better job of it than you could ever do yourself.

Chapter Eleven

Spirit Mates vs. Soul Mates

*I*know you are just ready for your soul mate already. A lot of people out there are looking for their soul mate, and I tell them what I'm about to tell you—you don't want just a soul mate. You also want a Spirit Mate. I realize the movies, songs, media, and literature of these modern times tell us that a soul mate is the highest form of love we can hope to have on the earth. We are indoctrinated that these connections are rare and only the luckiest of people find their twin flame, their "person," or as the character Phoebe told us on the television series *Friends*, "their lobster."

But lobsters aren't as rare as you think they are; in fact, there's an ocean full of them. Which is why every time you have a breakup, the older people in your life, the ones who have been around the block more times than you, say things like, "Don't worry, there are more fish in the sea." They know from experience that fish and lobsters are a dime a dozen. You can get one anywhere.

I could go down to the Piggly Wiggly right now and find you a soul mate. Unless you only eat organic produce, and then I would take you over to Whole Foods, but you get the point. Soul mates aren't rare; they are, in fact, in full supply.

You Are a Spirit, Who Lives in a Body and Possesses a Soul

To explain what a Spirit Mate is versus a soul mate, we need to get down to the basics. You are a spirit—you have a soul, which is the master control of your conscious and unconscious life (your mind, will, and emotions)—and you live in a body. Your spirit is the real you; your body is how your spirit interacts with the world, and your soul is the interface between the two.

Your soul is also known as your heart. It's that part of you where you have been filling in the cracks in the foundation and chasing all the little foxes out.

You are reading this book right now and processing it through your soul. If your soul is under the influence of cracks and foxes, it will listen to them more than to your spirit, which is the real and most trustworthy part of you. Your soul is what makes the daily decisions and runs the show.

Your unhealed soul (or unhealed heart) is not a great showrunner. It's what ran the crap show your life has been up until now.

Unfortunately, misery loves company and so do unhealed souls.

Soul mate attraction isn't inherently bad, but it means that your connection is based on feelings, thoughts, and other things that are subject to change. Soul mates *only* connect in the natural realm. The reality around you that you can see, touch, taste, and smell. These connections are based on and fueled by physical human attraction. It's what we often refer to as "chemistry." Chemistry can be gauged by things in common (both good things and negative things): taste in music, movies, or art; sense of humor; hobbies; shared past experiences; worldviews; and so on.

Spirit Mates are different from soul mates in that it is your spirit, that part of you that is unchanging and eternal, that is drawn to another. It creates something so strong that even a bad argument, a recession, a rough year, a lost job, or a chronic illness can't break it.

Spirit Mates connect at the soul level as well, but they also connect at a deeper level, an unexplainable level, an "I don't know; he's not usually what I like in a guy, but I just really like him" level. The connection is often supernatural and unexplainable by human reasoning.

You want to have a soul connection with your partner for sure, but soul connections—sexual attraction, the warm fuzzies, butterfly feelings, and so forth—can grow. Spirit connections need to be there from the beginning.

Who's That Guy?

I told you I walked out into my front yard and met my husband, but that's not the whole story. More than two years before that fateful day, I had gone to an event at a local megachurch. This church was not my church, and I had never been there before except once for a national conference.

Even though it wasn't my church, I had many friends and acquaintances who have attended this church over the years. One of these friends invited me to attend that day, and I reluctantly did.

If you haven't caught on yet, I'm not that big on church events or really any events that require you to put on real pants and leave your house. I'm usually the person who's really late to your party because I spent at least an hour trying to decide if I had to come. I like people, I really do, and for that reason I showed up at my friend's request.

This event was one of those outreach-to-the-community events that big ministries put on to attract new families to their congregation. It was called "Picnic with the Pastor," and it was quite an experience.

I attended a small, family-style church at the time, so I was amazed at this carnival-style event complete with rides, petting zoo, barbeque pit, and a large jumbotron playing funny videos. They had gone all out.

It was particularly the huge jumbotron that caught my attention. The videos that were being shown were prank videos that the staff of the church had played on one another. They were created in the style of a popular show on MTV at the time called *Punk'd*. Basically, the staff put together unbelievable scenarios and then made the person being "punked" think it was really happening. Right before the person broke down or lost their cool, they'd say, "Ha ha—fooled you."

They were well done and quite funny. The last video they played right before I left caught my eye in a different way. As I watched the prank unfold, I couldn't shake the idea that I knew the man in the video.

I began to rack my brain about where or in what context I had met him, but I couldn't make the connection. I began to question my friend. "Who's that guy?" I asked.

"Oh, that's so and so, our youth pastor," she responded.

Nope, that didn't ring a bell. "Where's he from, how old is he? Do you know where he went to school?" I pressed her for more information.

"I don't know," she said, now looking at me quizzically. "Why? He's married," she added.

I laughed. "That's fair," I said, "but I'm not asking for that reason." And believe me, I wasn't. I was on the back nine of a twelve-year marriage that was already 100 strokes over par and had three par 5s complete with water hazards still to go. The last thing I was interested in was men. "I just know him from somewhere," I explained. "I mean, I *really* know him; we must have gone to school together or something because he's very familiar to me."

It wasn't until we were cleaning out a garage two years into my marriage to David, four years after that church event, that we found that prank recording and I realized I'd seen David for the first time on that jumbotron. My draw to him at the time wasn't sexual. At the time, he was a dorky-looking guy with ill-fitting glasses and definitely was not my type.

But I felt a connection to him that I couldn't explain. This didn't stop me from yelling at him a couple years later when we met face to face, but Spirit Mate connections are like that—they defy reasoning.

Familiar Can Be Both Bad and Good

There's good familiarity and there's bad familiarity. As you just learned in the law of attraction, often we can be viscerally attracted to something that is the *opposite* of what we want. So when you feel a strong instant physical attraction, be very careful.

I can't tell you how many times I've helped pick up the pieces after someone went 100 miles an hour down the dead-end road of instant chemistry.

"It just felt like we've known each other forever," these women will say. "He told me on the first date he thought he was falling in love."

Hold up. Stop the car. What?

Yes, that guy seems familiar because you've already dated twenty versions of him. Remember? No? Okay there was Eric, Nathan, Josiah . . . oh, I see it's all coming back to you now. This type of instant chemistry can almost be like a drug. It can make us lose our senses and do stupid things such as ignore all the red flags blowing in our faces. I know you don't want to hear it, but it's called "lust" and it usually leads to bad decisions and walks of shame.

Shonda Rhimes and E.L. James would have us believe that instant physical attraction is a good thing, but it rarely, if ever, is. Do you want to jump a guy's bones while knowing absolutely nothing about him? Get a bucket of ice water if you have to but take a step back.

Let's check you before you wreck you, sister. It might be fun for a bit, but you can't build a lasting relationship or a marriage on just sexual attraction.

> This type of instant chemistry can almost be like a drug. It can make us lose our senses and do stupid things such as ignore all the red flags blowing in our faces.

It's Kind of Like *Déjà Vu*

When I say Spirit Mates are familiar, I mean it is right outside of your memory somewhere. You just can't place it, but there is an "ah-ha" feeling when you are with this person.

That's because they are already written into the Book of You that God wrote before the foundations of time. God has placed eternity inside us, meaning that there is a part of us that exists outside of time.

You probably won't know instantly when you find your Spirit Mate but as you get to know them, things will be different than they have been before. There will be a deep, foundational connection that you have never experienced. Instead of drawing you away from God, this connection will draw you closer and closer to the source of the love you're experiencing with each other.

Codependent Soul Mates

Okay, I will admit that the word "codependent" gets used too much (kind of like "narcissist"). It sounds scary, kind of like it belongs in the same category with words such as "deformed," "inbred," or "leprosy." Codependency is quite common and doesn't always look scary. It can even look healthy.

Codependency just means a relationship is formed on a spoken or unspoken contract. You are looking to each other to meet a specific need. Once that need no longer exists or you are no longer able to meet that need, the relationship dies—that death can happen quietly like in an Adele song or loud and messy like anything on the playlist from Ms. Swift.

Imagine a woman—we'll call her Lucy—is going on a first date with a man—we'll call him Steve. Lucy is quiet and doesn't like to rock the boat. She's not really into Steve but doesn't want to hurt his feelings by leaving.

They order dinner and Lucy continues to listen politely to stories about Steve's latest accomplishments at work. Finally their food comes, but it's cold and ill-prepared. Lucy doesn't say anything because she hates confrontation and doesn't want to cause a fuss.

Lucy takes a deep breath and prepares to white-knuckle her way through the plate of cold food when Steve says, "Hey, this food is cold. It must have been sitting in the kitchen for awhile." Steve calls the waiter back and politely but assertively makes the waiter bring him and Lucy a new order.

Well, now Lucy is super into Steve. He just did the thing she wasn't willing to do for herself. She now knows she can depend on him to have the backbone she doesn't have when conflict arises.

This kind of thing happens all the time. We are drawn to people who meet a specific need for us, and we attach ourselves to them, treating them as our sources of happiness, security, or whatever we feel we are lacking instead of God. Lucy and Steve might be able to have what appears to be a great relationship based on this foundation—at least for a while. They might even make it work long enough to get married and have a few kids.

But what do you think will happen if Lucy ever learns to have healthy confrontations with others for herself, or if

Steve doesn't like having a woman who doesn't need him to speak for her? The basis for their relationship will be gone and their "love" will fade.

Contract vs. Covenant Marriages

I run into couples all the time who want to get divorced not for reasons of abuse or infidelity, but for reasons of loss of interest and connection. They say things like, "I think I married the wrong person" or "I love them, I'm just not *in love* with them anymore." Give me a break.

In this generation of celebrity "conscious uncoupling but remaining best friends and co-parents," I call bullcrap. This is a perfect example of a soul mate relationship that didn't go any deeper. While I do believe there is hope for people who got married as soul mates, both people have to be willing to work at it.

These are what I call "contract marriages." They are relationships based in codependency. It's about meeting the needs of each other as the other person's source instead of coming alongside each other with God as your mutual source.

And this is why we say at weddings, "What God is putting together, let no human or thing ever separate again." So for those of you who are divorced, I want to ask you this: Was it really God bringing you together? Or did codependency bring you together? Was it a covenant or contract? Was God the source for both people? Was it interdependent? Was it the divine masculine and divine feminine coming back together?

The problem is that God isn't the one joining most marriages today. Codependency is.

There is a contract, though both people are usually so deep in counterfeit identities that they don't realize it. What do people usually say when they decide they've found the "one"? They say "He/she makes me happier than I've ever been."

While you should be happy to be with your future spouse, what's going to happen if they ever stop making you happy? You need something for the long term.

You want Mr. Right, not Mr. Right Now. A man might meet an immediate need, but will he fit the person you will be in ten, fifteen, or thirty years? Will there be room for the two of you to grow in intimacy? As it is, even Spirit Mates will run into difficulty.

> There will be moments when you tell yourself out of fear that it's time to let them go, but that will be when it's time to let them in even more.

You will hit soulish walls, even with Spirit Mates There will be times you want to cut and run. There will be times you want to smother him in his sleep. There will be obstacles to deeper intimacy as the two of you come closer over time. There will be moments when you tell yourself out of fear that it's time to let them go, but that will be when it's time to let them in even more.

People who have a Spirit Mate connection, unlike people who only have a soul mate connection, are able to do that deeper work, stay together, and overcome obstacles. They are the ones who are able to "fall back in love" and make it last for the long haul.

You're Making a List and Checking It Twice

Some people get so caught up chasing soul mates, they miss out on their Spirit Mates Other people are keeping everyone—good and bad—well away unless they meet a laundry list of qualifications. Enter the "lists."

Let's talk about lists for a bit. You know exactly what I'm talking about—your husband list. Lots of single women's workshops, ministers, books, and even friends will tell you to make one. You write the list, pray over it, repeat it every day, and you're supposed to attract the man who meets all the specs you've neatly laid out for God.

He'll be 6 feet 2 inches tall with blue eyes, six-pack abs, and a worship leader. His favorite movie will be *Pride and Prejudice*. He'll have a credit score over 800, and he'll have a successful job but will be home by 5:30 p.m. every night. He'll always smell like Old Spice, never fart in front of you, and always put the toilet seat down. He'll be an expert-level masseuse, play the guitar, and have no female friends or coworkers at all, ever.

While the principle behind lists is valid (we've covered the law of attraction and all that), most of the time lists are for self-protection. If a guy doesn't meet one of our list requirements, we immediately have an excuse to write him off. Lists often are just an elaborate self-defense mechanism created by those broken places in your heart.

I'm Not Going to Settle

I have a friend who is one of those women people always tell, "You're such an amazing catch! I don't understand how someone like you could be single. How are you not married yet?"

And they were right. She was quite a catch. She had everything going for her that a man could possibly want or admire in a woman. She was beautiful, intelligent, talented, but also kind, compassionate, and generous. She would make the perfect wife.

From the moment I met her several years ago, I really wanted to help her find her husband. We would have conversations through the years about what she was looking for in a man and, yes, like most women in their mid-thirties who had never been married, she had a list.

It wasn't an extensive list, and she convinced me that she wanted to be a wife and a mother more than anything else, but despite her age she was in no hurry because she refused to settle. I encouraged her to let go of her list, but she was adamant. Every year that she was single, it seemed to grow. Like most women, the older she got, the more she got used to being single.

As she watched other people her age make below-average matches in their hurry to the altar, she gripped that list even tighter. She even said what many single women (and men) in their 30s, 40s, and 50s say to me: "If I'm gonna get married now, they are going to have to be spectacular." She would meet someone, talk for a couple of weeks, and decide they just weren't tempting enough to give up her comfortable life as a single woman.

Then one day I met *him*. The list guy. He was everything she had written. He had the perfect resume for the open position as her husband. I called her immediately.

"What! No way!" she said.

"Yes, way!" I said. "He has every last thing on your list, and he's kind, generous, and handsome to boot."

Her reaction was more lackluster than I had anticipated. "Isn't this great news?" I asked. "Aren't you excited?"

"Yes, this is awesome!" she replied.

I wasn't buying it. She seemed more anxious than excited, but I just chalked it up to being nervous to meet the man of her dreams (or at least the man of her list).

I got her permission to give him her phone number and I waited to watch the fireworks fly. A few days later, I'd heard nothing. No Roman candles, not as much as a sparkler. What happened?

I called him first. "How's it going?" I asked.

"It's not going at all," he replied. "She said she was busy and couldn't talk until next week."

What? I knew she wasn't busy. I called her right away. "What's up? This is your list guy! I thought you would already be engaged by now," I joked.

"I'm just not feeling it," she said.

"What do you mean you're not feeling it? You haven't even talked to him yet."

"I know, but he seems too eager," she responded.

What in the world? Too eager? The biggest complaint I hear from women is that men don't pursue, and now trying to set up a phone call is too eager? What's really going on?

God Will Call Your Bluff

As we began to unpack the reasons behind this sudden avoidant and incongruent behavior, we discovered why she was in no hurry to meet the man who had everything she had always said she wanted. She was comfortable being single. She wasn't crying about it anymore. She had sat down at the table for one, realized she could order whatever she wanted off the menu, and she kind of liked it.

She still wanted to be married and have children, but she was finally at the place where she wasn't going to die if it never happened. She didn't want to go back. She wasn't expecting the list to come to life and text her, and she didn't know how she felt about it.

I realized that God was calling her bluff. She said she wanted this, but she had stopped believing that it was really going to happen. I convinced her at least to have a conversation with him. She did, and she didn't like him at all. Yes, she admitted he had everything that she had put on her list, but when you build a man in your imagination, he doesn't always look the greatest after it comes to life. I mean, look at Frankenstein.

> Sometimes it's not called settling for less. Sometimes it's just called surrendering for more.

This experience caused her to throw away the "I deserve only the best since I've been waiting so long" list. She ended up going out with a cute guy from her spiritual community who had been making googly eyes at her for more than a year. She had known he was interested, but he wasn't her ideal guy on paper, so she never gave him any encouragement to proceed. After all, she wasn't going to settle!

Ever since that first coffee date they have been inseparable and now, at the time of this writing, they are engaged to be married. Sometimes it's not called settling for less. Sometimes it's just called surrendering for more.

Is That List Really What You Want? Or Is It Just What You *Don't* Want?

Emmy is a client of mine who had four copies of her "list," and they were not working out for her. She was just as single as she'd always been with no one who even remotely resembled the person described on her list anywhere in sight.

After a few weeks with me, she burned all four copies of her list. (With actual fire on her back porch. It was quite spectacular.)

Emmy began to date guys outside her list specs—guys who were a little shorter, not quite as blond, fell a little further outside her religious background, and who came from different professions. But Emmy still had an internal list she was keeping, one called "not Dad."

Emmy's father is a former Marine. He's built like a linebacker and has a voice like a foghorn. His picture could be in the dictionary next to "All-American Manly Man's Man." Emmy was close with her dad as a kid and he was never abusive, but growing up Emmy had often been silenced, overruled, or even shouted down with that "I am the head of the house" line like a lot of kids from conservative families.

Because of this, Emmy assumed outspoken, passionate men like her dad were also aggressive, controlling, and insensitive.

So Emmy was going around on the dating apps and met guys through friends, but she was still checking them all against the internal list she kept. She was going on almost every date, but she was still dating a specific type of guy, ones who met the "not Dad" list criteria.

She was doing this consciously, by the way. She just assumed that anyone who was anything like her dad wasn't going to be compatible with her. Even though she had let go of the things on her written list, she found excuses to keep this one.

What happened? Emmy had met a great guy whom she really liked and who really liked her. She enjoyed talking to him and was pleased to find that he was nothing like her dad. This guy was smart, funny, and gifted, and it seemed like a very promising relationship.

The guy lived halfway across the country from Emmy, so she hopped on a plane and visited him for the weekend. They had a great time, and she flew home.

Then nothing. The guy didn't seem any more interested in talking to her than he had been before, and while she was there, she didn't get anything more affectionate than a side hug.

Emmy came back confused and wondering if she had been friendzoned. She called the guy about a week later for a "define the relationship" talk. Emmy's guy said that, yes, he was attracted to her. He even said she was pretty much everything he'd want if he had his own "wife list," but he was not sure if his feelings were strong enough for a relationship.

This was three months after their initial introduction. They'd talked several hours at a time multiple times a week and had spent a whole weekend together in person.

The guy was willing to keep talking and see if things went anywhere, but Emmy's feelings were way ahead of his. She decided she couldn't work with his lack of reciprocation, and she ended up calling things off.

So what happened?

Emmy's internal list of "not Dad" meant that she went for someone who, instead of being overbearing and aggressive, had the opposite problem. Emmy's list made her choose someone passive and emotionally unavailable, someone who wouldn't take risks. Emmy was so afraid of ending up with Dad 2.0 that she veered off in the opposite direction.

Her "list" had just one item on it, but it was still very much based on self-protection and just like her other, carefully bulleted list, it got her nowhere.

Nonnegotiables vs. Lists

There are some things on which you absolutely should not compromise. Abuse, violence, cheating, manipulation, and all things of that nature are definitely unacceptable in a relationship. Beyond that, each of us has custom nonnegotiables. We each have things that are unique to us that we must have in our lives.

Maybe you have a custody arrangement and can't move by order of the courts. Or perhaps you don't yet have children, but you *really* want to and you need a husband who wants children too. Maybe you feel called to serve in Syria and whomever marries you will have to be cool with that.

My husband, David, and I are very entrepreneurial and have been self-employed for much of our lives together. The ups and downs inherent to that calling aren't for everyone. What's now a nonnegotiable for us might be a deal breaker for many other people.

Rhett is a male client of mine who is sixty years old but looks forty-two. He is active, health-conscious, and works out so much, I get tired just thinking about it. One of Rhett's nonnegotiables is he wants someone who is active and healthy.

Many women (and men) whom I mentor in match-making will tell me not to introduce them to someone who is overweight or not in shape, but they are overweight and not in shape themselves. That's hypocrisy. If you're demanding that your person be something, my first question is if you are that thing.

In Rhett's case, it's not hypocrisy, it's about compatible lifestyles. It's not about finding a trophy wife, it's about someone who can keep up with him and be the companion for his golden years. He's close to retirement, but he's got a lot of life yet to live!

I'm very happy to say that Rhett recently started dating a wonderful lady he met at his gym. They are doing very well, and all indicators are pointing toward marriage.

If nonnegotiables come from your lifestyle, your calling, or facts about your life you cannot change, that's one thing. If it's just your own prejudices and assumptions, that's another.

One nonnegotiable many women have is height. Oh, my gosh . . . they get so hung up on *height*! You think your man needs to be tall enough to tuck you under his chin and make you feel all cute and little and snuggly.

I'm a tall girl. I'm 5 feet 10 inches tall. My husband is two inches shorter. If I had let height be a nonnegotiable, I would have missed out on the incredible love story we have lived for the past fifteen years. He's an amazing man who loves and cares for me and has turned out to be the best thing that I never even knew I wanted.

So stop being prejudiced against short guys. (Yes, I said it, prejudiced.) It's not their fault how long their legs are, and in case you hadn't considered this, it doesn't matter how tall you are when you're lying down.

If you're going to have nonnegotiables, make sure they are from God and not based on "lists," self-defense mechanisms, or your idea of how things "should" be. Everything else after those God-given deal breakers needs to be negotiable.

Chapter Twelve

"I Just Want..."

*B*elieve it or not, all the time I hear people say, "I just want someone who loves Jesus." I hear this not just from single women but from single men too (except they add, "And she's gotta be hot"). As many people as there are with their soul mate attractions and their lists, I have just as many people tell me they have one and only one deal break-er—"They just need to love Jesus."

No, he doesn't just need to love Jesus. Carl loves Jesus— you know, the guy who goes to your gym and still lives in his mom's basement? You can love Jesus and still be a hot mess. You can love Jesus and still not be mature enough to be in a romantic relationship, have bad hygiene, or still hang out with the guys all night playing video games. Just because someone checks "Christian" on their census form doesn't tell you a whole lot about their character.

Don't give guys a free pass on character and matu-rity just because you met them in church. Each of us has a unique gift and calling in life. God had a dream, and he wrapped your body around it before sending you into the world to do something worthy of your one and only life.

There is something you were put on this planet to do for the sake of God's grand design. Your divinely chosen husband is a part of that. If the two of you are going to both manifest your God-given potential, you need to share Destiny DNA.

Destiny DNA

What I call Destiny DNA can look different for different couples. It doesn't mean you need to have the same job, sense of style, or preferred thermostat setting, but it means you need to be headed in the same direction.

If a man wants to move to Africa to build water wells for the rest of his life, but you feel called to local politics, it's probably not a good fit. If he wants nothing to do with ministry, but you've dreamed of ministry your whole life...yeah, probably not.

Your careers don't have to be the same, but they need to be compatible. This looks different for everyone, but you need a shared vision, a shared goal.

Do you both have a dream to see young people reach their highest potential? Maybe he does that by being a high school football coach and you do it by being a volunteer at an after-school program. Either way, you are working toward the same goal.

> You don't have to have the same history with God, but you have to share the same destiny.

Like I've mentioned, David and I are both very entrepreneurial. We start and grow businesses together. We're self-employed. We share a passion for the restoration and healing of marriages and families. Those are all Destiny DNA things we share, despite our vastly different backgrounds and professions at the time we met.

Sharing Destiny DNA is about where you are going, not where you've been. You don't have to have gotten here by the same road, but you must take the same road moving forward. You don't have to have the same history with God, but you have to share the same destiny.

It is about growing together. You don't need someone who is as educated or as outwardly spiritual as you. You need someone who is teachable and willing to grow.

Equally Yoked

Ugh. Here's another phrase that gets in the way of so many women—equally yoked. "Don't marry someone unless you're equally yoked!" says the pastor as he tries to talk his head children's volunteer out of dating that cute guy from her work.

The phrase "equally yoked" comes from one of the Apostle Paul's letters where he warns against being "unequally yoked" in marriage. (I know by this time you probably think I have a bone to pick with Paul, but the poor guy can't help that his teachings have been so misinterpreted. It's been a long time, after all.) That passage is talking about believers marrying unbelievers. It's not talking about people from another denomination, people who can't quote as many verses as you, or the length of time someone has known Jesus.

I hear women tell one another all the time, "Don't marry potential!" That's bad advice, and it doesn't even make sense. What else is there? Nobody in this world has fully arrived.

Jesus is the only one who reached his potential here on Earth. So many women have this ridiculous idea that the man God has for them is going to be perfect like Jesus. Because of this, they are passing up the mere mortals with flaws who are all around them.

Well, if you want to marry perfection, I'll ping your phone when Jesus gets here. But those of you who want to get married now will need to marry potential. Every guy you meet will have an area, and probably two or three, that he needs to grow in, but it's not like you've arrived either. Hopefully, you're still growing too.

This entire Earth journey is about growth. If you are an eternal being, your time on earth can be considered your childhood. You're here to learn and to evolve. We are meant to fall down and scrape our knees a bit and get back up and try again. We are here to learn how to love and be loved. When you're really committed to growing and learning, you will be able to recognize that same desire in another person, even if you meet them just as they are brushing off their freshly skinned knees. You won't see their last mistake; you will see the hunger they have to learn from it and become a better version of themselves. There's a difference between seeing the real potential in someone and seeing fantasy. Fixer-uppers are for houses, not spouses. You don't want to try to stay in a dysfunctional relationship in the name of potential or put yourself or your children in a bad spot because "he can change."

It's vital that we begin to believe this because so many people hang on to a mistake because they think it's their

> There's a difference between seeing the real potential in someone and seeing fantasy. Fixer-uppers are for houses, not spouses.

only shot. They will stay in an abusive marriage or stay with the father of their children "because it's the right thing to do," even though the situation is dangerous and destructive to their emotional, spiritual, mental, and maybe even physical well-being.

We hear and say so often, "You have to lie in the bed you made." I believed that for a long time, staying in an unloving and unchanging marriage because I didn't want to admit defeat or failure. I didn't want to be "divorced." I believed the lie that if I ended my marriage, I would lose any future I had with God.

> Men were created to embody a different aspect of God and so they experience God differently.

I was being told that by many well-meaning Christian voices, and I believed them for twelve long and hard years, until my mental and physical health badly deteriorated while I was trusting God to "save my marriage." I was in and out of doctor's offices and emergency rooms as my mind and body paid the price for refusing to sign the "do not resuscitate" order on something I didn't want to admit did not have any more potential.

I'm not an advocate for divorce. I think it should be a last resort, but for really unhealthy matches like mine, where you just keep hurting each other over and over again with no end in sight, sometimes it's absolutely the only option.

You *do* want to see the good in someone that is already there. That doesn't mean he has to come to you fully actualized. It means he has to have the ability and the willingness to grow alongside you with the character to desire and to sustain that growth.

Fruit Inspectors vs. Gift Inspectors

We have to have our own relationship with God through Jesus. No one can have a relationship for you. The evidence of a relationship is its fruit—love, joy, and peace. Nothing external can give that to you. That can only come internally as the result of knowing God personally.

Gifts, on the other hand, are irrevocable. God gives them, and that's it. He doesn't take them back. A lot of people can mistake or confuse gifts and fruit.

A guy can be an awesome pastor or a passionate worship leader and still kick puppies in his private life. On the other hand, a guy who is kind, cheerful, and stays late at work to help a coworker with a flat tire might not be the most outwardly spiritual, but he does display more fruit.

One thing I hear men accused of a lot is not being as spiritual as women. I touched briefly on that earlier, but I just want to tell you again that's not true. Men were created to embody a different aspect of God and so they experience God differently.

The church has, over the past seventy years, come to be extremely feminized. Just look at the color palettes and prevailing décor choices in our church buildings to confirm that.

Don't hold it against a guy if he's not as pious in his church attendance or as outwardly expressive of his spirituality as you. There are men who pray out loud or cry during worship, but most of them will engage their faith in what appears to us as a more reserved, quiet way.

For too long, we've covertly or overtly heaped shame on guys because they don't express their spirituality the same way as women do. We've held up emotional cryfests, raised hands, and all-night prayer meetings as the ideal. There's nothing wrong with those things. I'm down for a good bawl-your-eyes-out worship service every now and again, but those things don't necessarily indicate that we have a healthy relationship with God. But patience, loyalty, and understanding certainly do.

Compatible vs. Combustible

You want a man, at least that's what I'm assuming. We want men, so it's important that we let men be men in these relationships. That sounds pretty obvious. But it's still something I have seen many women struggle with.

Often female clients explain to me what they want in a partner, and I'm like, "So ... you want to marry a woman?" They want someone who's sensitive, caring, in tune with their emotions, has perfect hygiene, is soft-spoken, likes to shop, and is down for mimosas with the girls anytime.

God made men different from women. While your husband should be your best friend, your closest confidante, and your most intimate earthly relationship, he's still going to be a man.

This isn't to say "boys will be boys" or that men can't learn emotional intelligence. It is to say that we need to stop judging these men by what women would do or how women would act.

Proverbs 18:22 is the basis for my men's relationship coaching program.

The man who finds a wife finds a treasure,
and he receives favor from the LORD.

—PROVERBS 18:22 NLT

When a man finds a wife, it's a sign of God's favor coming into his life and continuing to come in his life. If you've ever seen a man meet his Spirit Mate something incredible happens. Gifts, talents, and even dreams and ambitions will be unlocked that you may not have known were even there. The same thing is true for women. I am not the same person my husband married fifteen years ago, and he is not the same person I married.

When you find your Spirit Mate things blossom that were dormant before. We have blossomed so much after getting married that I tell people we are no longer the dormant Dormans. We have no idea what these men could become until we see them in a healthy covenant relationship with a Spirit Mate. So we need to stop judging them by what they have been able to become alone, without their feminine counterparts, their ezers. Don't underestimate the influence of a healthy, whole-hearted woman in the life of a man. There are a lot of things men will grow into, but we need to accept that in some ways, they will always be different from us..

Divine Masculine and Divine Feminine

Before all that "dis" that came after the garden, the masculine and feminine enjoyed a divine unity. Marriage is about the divine masculine and the divine feminine coming back into the unity we were always meant to have. It's two complementary opposites reuniting.

You want someone who is a complementary opposite, able to counterbalance you while creating synergy with your unique gifts and talents. That's compatibility.

You can be the boss babe, kicking ass and taking names at work, but when you come home, you need to leave that at the office. You're not your husband's boss. You're his equal, his partner. Healthy men are not looking for drill sergeants, nurses, or sugar mommies. They are looking for wives— women who will boldly embody the divine feminine to bring the divine masculine out of them. Don't hear what I'm not saying. I am a strong woman and a thought leader, and my husband loves every bit of it. He respects and admires me and is not the least bit intimidated by me. Why is that? Because I'm just being who I am. This is how God made me and because I didn't try to hide that when we met, he knew exactly what he was getting himself into (unlike my first marriage where I was trying to be whatever I thought he wanted me to be). You can't have an intimate relationship with this type of dishonesty. You can't keep up with a counterfeit forever. The true definition of a relationship is that it can't be good for you if it's not also good for me. That's why it's so important to have a healthy heart. If you do, you will own your identity without trying to overcompensate for what you're not or make apologies for what you are.

A healed, healthy, and whole heart is super sexy to a man who is looking for a wife. She is vulnerable, open, and receptive. She is God-defended so she doesn't need to be self-defended. You know we don't have to look very far to know we're the receiver. Just take a look at your anatomy down south. Your vajay-jay is designed to receive.

> A healed, healthy, and whole heart is super sexy to a man who is looking for a wife.

You were created to be vulnerable, welcoming. When we are hard, bitter, and closed off, that's not attractive to a man who is looking for a wife. Some of you have been trying really hard to become a bride. Lily Tomlin is quoted as saying, "If you tried harder and that didn't work, try softer." A man looking for a wife is looking for a woman who can be strong and soft, someone who will receive what he has to offer and give back something greater. A woman who can accept his gift of being able to protect and provide, not a woman who doesn't need him and can do everything herself.

If a man is attracted to your counterfeit masculine aggression, he's not looking for a wife. He's looking for a roommate, someone to have sex with, and maybe even someone to help pay the bills—but not a wife. Men who want wives want someone who will be the yin to their yang, someone they can protect and care for.

The divine feminine and masculine are complementary opposites at their finest, two sides of the same coin.

Here are some divine feminine traits:
- **Nurturer**
- **Counselor**
- **Intuitive**
- **Comforter**
- **Vulnerable**
- **Soft**
- **Receptive**
- **Wise**

And here are some divine masculine traits:
- **Order keeper**
- **Identity giver**
- **Protector**
- **Provider**
- **Covering**
- **Defender**
- **Loyal**
- **Dispenser of justice**

You'll notice there's nothing on these lists about who makes more money, who works, who stays at home with the kids, who handles the money, or anything else our culture stereotypically defines as gendered. This isn't about gender roles, the color clothes you wear, or how well you can apply winged eyeliner. It's about identity. Men are looking for these feminine traits in a wife because if they are a healthy man, they are already bringing the masculine traits to the table. Go ahead and be that strong feminine leader at work, in the community, at church, or anywhere else that you have been called to lead people—both men and women. But when you come home, be able to lean into your husband. You can exhale, and just be soft and open and receive his love and protection.

To recap, you want a Spirit Mate—someone who shares your Destiny DNA, someone you can build a soul mate connection with, whom you enjoy and love to be around, and someone who meets your nonnegotiables but doesn't "just" love Jesus. You need someone who can grow with you, not just someone who fits who you are right now.

Your Spirit Mate will be someone who isn't exactly like you but who has the things you don't have, so when you work together as a team you both win. Polar opposites may attract, but they don't cohabitate for very long. Fire and ice make for fun cocktails, but trust me when I tell you, they don't make for good marriages.

Chapter Thirteen

Becoming
the Bride

*I*n this day and age, it's easy to feel like we've been created for loss, hurt, and pain, but that's not the truth. You were created for love, and so was I.

We are going to have a hard time believing that right away. We have been repeating the opposite to ourselves for so long. I want you to say this out loud right now: "I was created for love." Say it again: "I was created for love."

Feel that warmth travel through you as your heart begins to receive that truth and pump it to every cell in your body.

"I was made to love and be loved."

Feel it circulating through your whole body, even passing through the blood-brain barrier like sweet molecules of grace bringing hope and peace to all the chaos in your soul.

"I was made to love and be loved."

While you do have to continue to allow the Holy Spirit to do the foundational heart work I've outlined in this book, you don't have to become a bride; you already are the bride. You are just un-becoming all the other stuff you are not. You can't do that on your own, but continuing to surrender these broken places to God will cause our hearts to become soft again and reveal God's greatest truth about who we are. Once that happens, the lives we've been born to live can finally get activated.

The real you has been hidden under all these counterfeit layers for a long time, and the Holy Spirit has come alongside you like the fairy godmother in the story of Cinderella to show you who you really are. God is saying to you, "I don't want to just clean up your outside identity, but only you can surrender the inside identity." He doesn't want you to lie there in those ashes anymore. He wants you to go to the ball, but he also wants you to believe in your heart that you belong at the ball. Otherwise, you're just a servant girl in a fancy dress.

No Longer Hidden

I know you have felt hidden, maybe even invisible, for so long. One of my students told me that men never paid attention to her before she started working with me. "You aren't invisible," I told her. "You're hiding." The shame of perceived and even real rejection can cause us to project a false insignificance to the world that tells everyone, "I'm not worth your attention." As my student continued in this process of coming out from under the layers of lies she believed about her own value, she began to notice a big change in how people treated her. She said, "Men notice me now! It's almost embarrassing. All kinds of men, young and old, have been smiling at me, opening doors for me, initiating conversation with me. I feel so seen for the first time in my life."

She was never invisible; in her heart she just believed she was invisible, and that is what she became as a result.

This Is Your Debut

In the "old days," they used to have events called debutante balls. I know, I know. Completely archaic. Women of marrying age were put on display for the purpose of making a profitable match. It's a tradition that I'm glad is no longer necessary, but I believe the people of that time did have the best intentions. They wanted a good marriage for their daughters, which during that time in history, was the only chance women had at a good life. Thank God that's not true today. Here's the way these "coming out" shindigs worked: The families would host parties when their daughter reached an age of maturity to reveal, or debut, her to the community to say, "This is our beautiful, accomplished daughter; we are very proud of her and she is now ready to be seen by the world." After her initial debut, she was considered eligible to be courted or to receive an offer of marriage from an interested suitor.

I believe it's time for your debut, and it's not about a fancy dress or a great pair of shoes. It's about God revealing *you*, his beautiful daughter, to the world.

You Are God's Daughter

It's important that we no longer think of marriage or motherhood as our purpose in life. While most women have been created for a destiny that includes marriage and family, our identity is not as a wife or mother—it's as a daughter. I went through a season where I was really struggling with my identity and purpose. When I asked God, "What is my purpose?" his answer was not what I expected. He said, "Your primary and most important purpose in this life is to be my daughter, and to show this world what a daughter of God looks like."

- **What do daughters of God look like?**
- **Daughters don't worry—they worship.**
- **Daughters don't strive—they surrender.**
- **Daughters don't hate—they celebrate.**
- **Daughters don't slave—they inherit.**

It doesn't always come naturally to us to be daughters. I know it didn't for me. I had a strained and hard relationship with my mother for most of my life, and a nonexistent relationship with my father. I am happy to report that is not the case today. My mom went to heaven eighteen months ago, but before she did, God healed my relationship with her beyond my wildest imagination. But for most of my life, I felt like an orphan. I didn't belong anywhere or to anyone. I always thought I was on the outside looking in. Like my former student, I felt insignificant and invisible. I felt envious of people who had strong connections to their family. It seemed as if they had better opportunities in life than I did because, in my opinion, they were more stable, confident, and prosperous than people like me.

So when God started calling me a daughter, it changed my whole life. Now, don't get me wrong, it didn't change my life overnight, or even in one year. I had a huge learning curve. Learning how to depend on a father was something I had never done in my life, and I didn't have anyone to teach me how so it was hard. Learning how to trust someone to take care of me and protect me was even harder. It took me years to surrender to being God-defended instead of self-defended, but Papa God was very patient with and loving to me in my process, and he will be with you too. My greatest hope is that with resources such as this book, it won't take you as long as it did me to believe you are a beloved daughter of God. When you do, it will change everything and prepare you like never before to receive everything God has always had for you, including the love of an amazing husband.

Progress, Not Perfection

The changing of your heart will be a process and it will take time. Using the spiritual revelation and tools that you learned in this book, you will continue to reclaim a healthy, healed, and whole heart. You didn't get in the place you're in overnight, and you won't get to where God wants to take you overnight. This book is titled *Married in 12 Months or Less*, not *Married in 12 Weeks or Less*.

The good news is that if you stick with this heart-healing process, you will start to see a dramatic change right away in the way you see yourself and in the way others see you. I get testimonies all the time from women just like you who tell me that coworkers are stopping them to say they are glowing and family members and friends are noticing how happy and "different" they seem.

As I've watched many women go through this change, I can say it looks like this—one huge shift followed by several smaller shifts, a period of adjustment to your new mindset, a couple small roadblocks, maybe a big roadblock, and repeat.

I know that doesn't sound like the most exciting road trip, but I know that you will really like the destination. There are moments, days, and maybe even weeks and months that won't be easy. But you can do this with the Holy Spirit's help.

New Beginnings Require Endings

Not everyone will be super excited about the changes they see in you. In fact, some people will be threatened by them, and they will respond with resistance and possibly even anger. People who have known you the longest may be the most unsupportive and uncomfortable with the *new* you. It's not uncommon for unhealthy families and communities to try to hold one another back with negativity and control. They may even verbally attack you by saying things such as, "Why do you want to get married, you're too old/young. This isn't like you, are you sure you're okay? I'm worried about you. You're acting weird. I don't like the new you."

Their discomfort stems from fear. Your life changes may inadvertently make them feel like they need to change, too, and they don't feel ready for that quite yet. You can't allow the opinions or fear of others to put you back in the waiting

202 | *Married in 12 Months or Less*

room. One of my current matchmaking clients comes from a long line of single women. She really wants to be married, and the women in her family seem supportive of that until she begins to get serious with a guy. As soon as she communicates that things are beginning to get serious, her mother and aunts, who are all single, start trying to sabotage the relationship and cast doubt over her choice of the man. It's like the story of the crabs in the bucket. If you put one crab in a bucket, it will eventually claw its way out, but if you put a bunch of crabs in the bucket, they will keep pulling one another down so that none of them ever gets out. The same mentality is behind this type of family or friend sabotage as they are basically saying, "If being single is good enough for me, it's good enough for you," or "If I can't have it, I don't want you to have it either."

> God didn't ask anyone's permission when he wrote the story of your life, and you don't need anyone's permission to live it.

Border Bullies

You can't allow the naysayers, even if they are people whom you love, to prevent you from living out the desires of your heart, whether that desire is to finish college, move to a new city, go after an unlikely but exciting childhood dream, or find the love of your life. God didn't ask anyone's permission when he wrote the story of your life, and you don't need anyone's permission to live it. You don't need permission from anyone to do that great thing that's in your heart. You want to know why? Because God already gave it to you. Especially when it comes to love and romance. He gave you the desire in your heart to be a wife, which means you're preapproved. You don't need to be validated by anyone else, you don't need their support, you don't need their approval, and you don't need their permission.

So many people are keeping themselves on the shelf waiting for someone to give them permission. If you do this, you might be waiting forever. It's time to move forward. It's time to take that step and give *yourself* permission to be who you want to be! Stop waiting for some other person, place, or thing to blow in your sails. Turn your sails to the wind and allow divine purpose to start blowing you in the right direction.

Rock the Boat

You're going to have to come to terms with the fact that not everyone is going to be on board with what God is speaking for you to do with your life. They might also include ones whom you choose to date and marry. Many people have voices in their lives they need to silence; those voices are keeping you from getting to where you are going. They are bringing stagnation to you. This doesn't mean all advice and advice-givers are bad. It just means it's dangerous to take advice from those who don't have a vested interest in the outcome. In other words, those who aren't invested in God's promises over your life don't have a say in what you do. So if you are one of those women like my client who is surrounded by a big, nosy family or group of friends who are always offering unsolicited advice, trying to make you feel afraid of stepping out and taking a chance, then you're probably going to have to get a little sassy with them.

You could try this: Carry your monthly bills around and when they insist you're living your life wrong, hand them one. Better yet, give them a few to choose from; when they object, just let them know since they are running their mouths and your life this month, you expect they will be paying your car note too. This is guaranteed to bring dead silence to the amateur "Judge Judy" in your life.

> So rock that boat and see who falls out…and whoever falls out, leave them there.

But seriously, honey, you better rock that boat. *Rock it!* You know why? Because some people need to fall out of your boat! You're trying to get them on board, but they really need to be out of your boat! So rock that boat and see who falls out…and whoever falls out, leave them there. I'm saying this from a place of love because you have to stop thinking that leaving people behind is a bad thing. If you want growth, if you want destiny, your life is going to have to have necessary endings, and they are one of them.

God has a love story for you. Let's get you ready to step into it.

Batter Up...

My youngest adult daughter was still living at home when the COVID-19 pandemic hit America. She was eighteen, almost nineteen, and because she was working as a nanny, she immediately lost her job.

The city where we live—Austin, Texas—quickly instituted a mandatory stay-at-home order, and the couple she worked for no longer needed a nanny. She really liked her job, and she was completely bummed to lose it. She knew that she wasn't going to be there forever, but it was a good job for that season of her life, and she really enjoyed the pay and flexibility it provided.

As everyone knows, the shutdown seemed to last forever. With everything closed except the big box stores, my daughter struggled to find another job. After months of being unemployed, she finally got a lead on a new job. It was, ironically, another job as a nanny.

The couple hadn't been forced to work from home like most people in the city, as their jobs were considered "essential." They were looking for someone who could start right away to care for their preschool-aged daughter. Their other nanny was moving soon, and they hoped she could teach the new nanny the ropes before she left.

After a phone interview, the couple decided to hire my daughter. She was really excited, partly because this job paid more than any job she had ever had before (and my girl loves to shop) and partly because she was stir-crazy from being quarantined. She couldn't wait to get back out into the world again.

The first couple of days went great. The mom and dad seemed professional but nice, and the little girl was very active, which made the day go by quickly. But on the third day of her first work week, something went wrong.

I woke up to the sound of the front door closing and I glanced at the clock—8:00 in the morning. Knowing that my daughter was supposed to be at her job by 7:45 and that she still had a twenty-five-minute drive, I called her phone.

Her voice was panicked. "I'm so late," she said. "I slept through my alarm, and I didn't wake up until fifteen minutes ago."

"Calm down and slow down," I replied. I instinctively knew as her mom that she was going to drive like a bat out of hell trying to time travel to somehow make up the fifteen minutes she was already late. "Better late than dead," I added.

"C'mon, Mom! Seriously, this is bad." She sounded as if she were about to cry.

This is the kid who never wanted to get in trouble at school. The girl who always did the right thing to avoid any type of conflict and confrontation. I can imagine that having to deal with an angry employer was probably her worst nightmare.

But this wasn't a weak area for her, and that's the truth. She was usually responsible and had never had any issues with time-management in the past. Knowing this, I tried to comfort her.

"You aren't usually a late person. It's going to be okay. Everyone is entitled to a one-off," I assured her.

She exhaled, "Okay, I hope you're right."

And like most mothers, I was right. I felt a peace in my heart that everything would work out fine, and it did. She got to work, apologized profusely to the mother who was now late to work herself, and was met with grace and mercy. Her employer let her know that she understood that sometimes these things happen and that she appreciated her getting there as soon as she could. My daughter breathed a sigh of relief, and the day went on as usual.

For the next couple of days, everything was great. My daughter loved her new job, which basically means she loved the idea of all the things that she was going to buy on payday, and all was right in her world.

Then it happened again.

I was at an early morning appointment when I got a frantic and distraught call from my daughter. She had forgotten to set her alarm again. She was so tired from a long day of childcare that she had gotten into bed and had fallen asleep without remembering to set it. She had texted her employer to tell them what had happened and to apologize but had not yet received a response. That's never a good sign.

She was on her way to work but she was going to be more than thirty minutes late. This was the second time she was going to be more than a half-hour late in her first week of work. I wanted to comfort her, but I knew in my gut this wasn't going to end like the first time. And it didn't.

This time the father was there to greet her when she knocked on the door. He informed her very civilly but coldly that they would no longer be needing her services. He then promptly shut the door, leaving my daughter completely devastated.

She had been fired from her job! She called me practically wailing. She was so upset. How could this happen? She had never been fired in her entire life (which is good since she's only had three jobs). From the way she was carrying on, you would have thought she had been fired after years of faithful service.

The rejection of the whole situation was more than her people-pleasing heart could handle. She had failed, and she just couldn't take it. I listened as her pendulum swung between Victim and Survivor and then back again at an amazing rate of speed.

"How could they do this to me?' she demanded through her tears. "That dad was so mean! He just closed the door right in my face! What a jerk! I can't believe how stupid I am! I am such a loser. I deserve this. Isn't there anything I can do to fix this? I wonder if the mother would give me another chance. This isn't like me. I'm not a late person. I've just developed really bad habits over the last six months in quarantine."

I had to admit that was true. Even though I thought it was a long shot, I could see that she wasn't ready to admit defeat and that she wasn't going to go down without a fight. "Why don't you text the mom and apologize, and see if she'd be willing to let you have one more chance?" I offered. "Do you think she will do that?" she asked hopefully. "I don't know, but it's worth a try," I responded.

I have known many professional families, and I know that they don't mess around when it comes to the level of excellence they expect from their caregivers. I also knew that my daughter was definitely not showing up as her best self, and if they gave her another chance, she wouldn't do this again. This family was very busy and didn't seem to have a backup nanny plan, which might work in her favor for another chance. So she gave it a shot.

What happened next is why I'm telling you this story.

My daughter texted the mother and told her everything that she had told me. That she was so sorry, that this behavior was not her norm, and that she had never had trouble with lateness before now. But throughout the quarantine she had developed some bad habits of staying up late and not using an alarm since there was nowhere to go. She told her boss that she loved the job and knew that if she gave her another chance, she could do a great job. She offered all kinds of feasible solutions to the problem: "I will set three alarms if needed. I will ask my parents to wake me up. I will do whatever I need to do to make sure this never happens again."

The mother responded very graciously. She thanked my daughter for her apology, she complimented her on how well she had performed her nannying duties the previous days of the week, and she assured her that she thought she was a great young woman.

But she didn't give her another chance.

Instead she told her that those were all great ideas to make sure she was on time from now on, but that she needed her to have done that before she took the job. She told my daughter that by accepting the job, it was expected that she would already be prepared and ready before she was hired. But the mother didn't stop there.

She also told my daughter that she believed my daughter would learn from this situation and be ready to show up as her best self the next time she got an opportunity. She said, "I believe in you, and the next time you get a chance like this, you're going to be successful."

It was a hard lesson to learn; it hurt, and my daughter didn't like it. But you know what? What that mother predicted is exactly what happened. My daughter was able to see her blind spots and weak areas through that experience. She decided that she was going to work on them so she would be ready the next time. And the next time around came fast! It didn't take long at all for her next opportunity to show up.

> It doesn't matter how many times you have been up to bat and struck out or if you've never been up to bat at all. You're up next and you're going to be ready to swing for the fences.

Within just two weeks of being let go at that job, she was offered another job, with even more responsibility. This time she was prepared! She showed up with everything she needed already in place, and she hit it out of the park!

It doesn't matter how many times you have been up to bat and struck out or if you've never been up to bat at all. You're up next and you're going to be ready to swing for the fences.

If we get hold of what God would like to teach us, it has the power to change our lives forever.

I'm not saying you still have to do all this work before you will be able to succeed at or attract a romantic relationship worthy of your Destiny DNA. I'm not saying that at all. I would be the last person ever to tell anyone anything like that.

To all of you who adhere to the idea of God's perfect timing—ha! I'm sure it's perfect somewhere in the universe, but to my linear view of life, the timing of my love story seemed anything but perfect.

The ink on the dissolution papers for my first marriage wasn't even dry when I walked out into my front yard and met my husband. You guys know how well that meeting went. But God knew more about me than I knew about myself. He knew my potential, and he saw my capacity to grow and change. He wanted to give me another chance at bat even though I had just struck out.

Even though from outside appearances, others may not think I deserved it, God saw my heart. He knew I had finally let go of the pen and was ready to let him write my new love story. I was done controlling my life, and I was done letting other people control my life too. I didn't want to be in charge anymore, and because of that surrender, he was able to become my matchmaker. He opened my husband's eyes to see the wife in me who was just waiting to be awakened by the love of a husband. He gave David the desire to be that husband and to walk through the healing process with me.

I had massive trauma wounds from a childhood of abandonment and abuse. Add to that over a decade in a rocky, codependent marriage and I knew I still had a lot of things to work through. But this man—this wonderful man who was gifted to me by God—stayed with me through all of that. He has helped me walk through my healing process, and I have helped him walk through his.

We both knew the other was far from perfect, and we still chose each other anyway.

Whole in Christ, Complete in Marriage, Healed in Family

"Jackie, are you saying I don't have to even be completely healed before I meet my husband?"

That's exactly what I'm saying. It's all about a heart posture of surrender—when you finally know that hole in your heart is a God-shaped hole. When you know it's not a man-shaped hole, a friend-shaped hole, a career-shaped hole, or any other kind of hole, you're ready.

The human resources department of Heaven wants to assign human assistance to help you heal.

Often the antidote to a poison is the very thing that poisoned you, but the remedy is mixed with other active ingredients. Ingredients such as forgiveness, repentance,

> Yes, it's true that broken people, break people and hurting people, hurt people.
>
> Those are true stories. But here's a story we don't tell often enough: healed people, heal people.

maturity, and revelation. Most of our hurt comes from relationships with people, so part of the way God heals us from bad relationships is with good relationships. If you were hurt in marriage, you will be healed in marriage. If you were hurt by friends and family, friends and family will be part of your restoration. Yes, it's true that broken people, break people and hurting people, hurt people. Those are true stories. But here's a story we don't tell often enough: healed people, heal people.

Love Is Spelled R-I-S-K

I have seen people choose each other in the face of the most dire and seemingly hopeless circumstances. It's a brave—or, some would say, stupid—thing to do to hitch your wagon to the train that looks like it's about to go off the tracks. But I watch people do it all the time as God plays matchmaker in their lives.

I have watched as healthy, successful men choose women who are battling health problems, sometimes very serious, life-threatening conditions. I have seen women choose men who have lost everything they own and have nothing to bring to the table financially. I've seen people persevere through long military deployments, mental health challenges, and visa/immigration struggles.

It's different when you're already married and life presents these kinds of challenges. You already signed up for better or for worse, but let's be honest—many married people do a disappearing act when things get hard.

But these couples chose hard times with each other. They signed up to go through life with each other when things were at their worst without even giving it a second thought. When God is the matchmaker, it doesn't matter what the obstacle is because together with God, they know they are more than a match to overcome it. Why? Because something much bigger than either one of them is at work in their lives, and they know it.

Chapter Fourteen

God's Plan Is Bigger than You

*I*t's important that you get hold of this right now—your marriage is mission critical. The truth is that God had a dream of something he wanted to do in the world, so he wrapped your body around it and sent you into this world. You have a calling and you have a destiny, and marriage is a part of God's plan to help you reach it. Marriage and family are God's greatest maturity plan for mankind. He uses them to mold us into our highest identity.

That destiny for which you were born is vital to all of us because only when we are all living in our full potential as sons and daughters of God, can we bring hope and healing to the world.

> Marriage and family are God's greatest maturity plan for mankind. He uses them to mold us into our highest identity.

David and I have seen thousands of people's lives transformed in our fourteen years together. Our marriage isn't just a marriage; it's an alliance between two people who are working together to advance his Kingdom on Earth. That's exactly what God told me when I asked him why he had brought us together.

You might be thinking right now, *Well, Jackie, that's great for you. You're a spiritual teacher and of course he's going to give you a supernatural love story.*

Well, not quite. You see, David and I know our marriage isn't about us, just like your marriage isn't about you. It's about something even bigger. I want to encourage you to ask God what purpose your future marriage holds. Allow him to begin to show you the bigger picture over your life than just what you can see now.

Even though God is making these matches, it's not always going to be fun. It's not going to be convenient. You will not always like the things you have to do to steward this gift of marriage. I don't know why we think the good relationships are the easy ones. *Good* and *easy* are not synonyms. I had easy teachers in school, you know, the type who never assigned any homework and let you have open book tests. I can't remember a thing those teachers taught me. But the more difficult teachers, the ones who challenged me, the ones who didn't let me off the hook but encouraged me to dig deep—*those* are the teachers who changed me.

Even as a happily married woman, I can promise that marriage is going to force you to change. It's going to bring things out of you that you didn't even know were there, good and not so good. We all know that iron sharpens iron, but we often forget that pieces of iron sharpen other pieces by rubbing off the other's rough edges. This is how the two become one; they make room for each other by losing some of themselves and together creating something new and even more beautiful.

All God Ever Wanted Was Family

All God ever wanted was a family. God wants to see you in a healthy marriage because he wants to put a union of the divine feminine and the divine masculine on display just like he did in the garden in the very beginning of this love story between God and mankind. He wants the world to see what his family was supposed to look like in its original form. For you to truly come into the fullness of everything God has for you, he needs you to experience earthly family. Part of that is experiencing love and relationship in marriage. If that is what God has placed in your heart to pursue, it is part of his destiny plan for your life.

> God is more into crockpots than microwaves. Almost every time when God gives us a promise, it comes with a process.

You don't have to be (and you won't be) completely healed or matured before you get married, but a lot of healing *can* take place before you meet your Spirit Mate. I believe the more you can do ahead of time, the better, but some things take processes, and some things require time spent in a healthy relationship. I've told you I was far from healed when I remarried, and as a result I spent the beginning of my marriage trying to convince David to reconsider his choice because I didn't do my heart work ahead of time. I want to make sure that you don't do that. I want you to be able to enjoy the amazing partner God is giving you without trying to talk yourself, or him, out of it.

Most of us do not experience healing as immediately as we would like. No, I don't like it either. Especially in our culture of microwaves, one-click downloads, and instant everything, we want to hit a button or flip a switch. We want what we want, and we want it now.

Unfortunately, God is more into crockpots than microwaves. Almost every time when God gives us a promise, it comes with a process. Even those "instantaneous" miracles are rarely instantaneous at all. Most of the time, they are the result of a process that was begun some time ago but has just now reached a tipping point.

You Don't Need Easy; You Just Need Worth It

Is it going to be easy? Probably not. I can tell you right now that there will be challenges and setbacks. Some of those challenges and setbacks will be external. They may come from circumstances, crazy exes, or disapproving family members. Others will be internal from you, the things you believe, and the filters you have as the result of trauma. My goal is to help you heal from the internal things that are holding you back so that you and the man God has picked to be your husband can overcome those external things together.

There will be times when you might want to call it quits like I did, but I encourage you to keep using what you have learned in this book, keep moving forward, and stay in the process God has for you.

You don't need easy; you just need worth it. I can promise you that the healed, whole, and healthy version of you that will come out in the marriage God has for you is worth it.

Ours is an amazing story of restoration and healing that came from the midst of brokenness. I believe God wants that same level of restoration and healing for you. Your story is customized to you, so even when your heaven-penned love story doesn't look the way the storybook says it should, it will look the way God says it should.

Remember, God doesn't write boring, mediocre love stories; he writes epic, world-changing adventures. Are you finally ready to trust him? If so, it's time to give him back the pen and let him write your story.

Unlock the Secret to Your Love Story

Are you ready to reclaim your love life, heal your heart, and unlock the secret to finding your Spirit Mate? Then sign up for Jackie Dorman's *Married in 12 Months or Less Challenge today* at LoveStories.com!

You can join the movement that is igniting change and bringing hope to men and women from all walks of life who are ready to step into the love story already written for them.

If you have taken the *Married in 12 Months or Less Challenge* and it has changed your life, we'd love to hear from you! Share your personal story now at:

To connect to Jackie, find out where she is speaking, or simply share how her teaching has impacted you, visit:

www.JackieDorman.com

Follow Jackie on:

FB: @jackiedormanofficial

IG: @jackiedormanofficial

Acknowledgments

*F*irst and foremost, I want to thank God for giving me a big mouth and always filling it with something worth saying. I love being on this adventure with you. You have blessed me beyond my wildest dreams, and I can't wait to see what happens next!

Endless thanks to my partners at Contagious Inc.: David Sams, Denise Payne, and Curtis Wallace. None of this would even be possible without you. Thank you for believing in me and helping me reach millions of men and women with this message. Here's to catching lightning in a bottle and impacting millions of lives together into the future.

A great *big* thank you to the M12M Home Team. You all are the real MVPS: Amber Hennigan, Kassandra Maggiore, Gabby Labatista, Bethany Stanko, Jessica Moore, Cheryl Guyong, Lorraine Finnicle, Candy Bleier, Liz Robertson, Brandi Scott, Danelle Shoemaker, and Natasha O'Neil.

Thank you to Jonathan Merkh, Jennifer Gingerich, Becky Philpott, Lauren Ward, and the incredible hard-working team at Forefront Books for taking on this project and holding my hand every step of the way. You guys made it easy!

And to Elisabeth Wheatley, thank you for the kick-ass outlines, transcribing endless videos of me talking, and for letting me sit on your couch and eat all your snacks for hours and hours every day. But mostly, thank you for helping me get everything I wanted to say out of my heart and onto the pages of this book.

My deepest love and thanks go to my adult children—Jaren, Kaylee, and Regan—for always encouraging me to keep going. Being your mom has been the greatest blessing and honor of my life. I love you with all my heart.

And last, but not least, I will forever be grateful for the amazing community of women who have connected with me over the years. You have encouraged me, supported me, and trusted me to teach, mentor, coach, and lead you. That means more than you will ever know.

From my very first women's event twenty-four years ago until now, you have continued to show up to everything and anything I have done. You read my *Real Life Unplugged* blog, came to my early-morning *WOW Women* prayer calls, helped me launch *Jane TV*, attended my *Heart Work* courses and *New You* workshops, and watched me every morning fumble around with my camera on *Wake Up Call with Jackie* on Periscope and Facebook Live.

We've come a long way, baby, and we've come together. We have prayed together, laughed together, cried together, and now through this "Married in 12 Months" marriage and family movement we are once again changing the world together. Thank you, my sisters, your loyalty and love mean the world to me.

Notes

1 B. A. D. Lendrem, D. W. Lendrem, A. Gray, J. D. Isaacs. "The Darwin Awards: Sex Differences in Idiotic Behaviour." BMJ, 2014; 349 (December 10, 2020), https://www.bmj.com/content/349/bmj.g7094.

2 "Traffic Safety Facts: Crash Stats," U.S. Department of Transportation, National Highway Traffic Safety Administration, https://crashstats.nhtsa.dot.gov/Api/Public/ViewPublication/812115.